The Compleat Crab and Lobster Book

The Compleat

Crab and Lobster Book

Revised and Updated Edition

Christopher R. Reaske

Illustrated by Suzanne T. R. Crocker

BURFORD BOOKS

Printed in the United States of America

10   9   8   7   6   5   4   3   2   1

Library of Congress Cataloging-in-Publication Data
Reaske, Christopher Russell.
    The compleat crab and lobster book / Christopher R. Reaske ;
illustrated by Suzanne T. R. Crocker.
        p.   cm.
    Includes bibliographical references and index.
    ISBN 1-58080-027-0 (pbk.)
    1. Cookery (Crabs).   2. Cookery (Lobsters).   3. Crabs.
4. Lobsters.   I. Title.
TX754.C83R43   1999
641.6′95—dc21   98-43873
                                             CIP

For Katharine, Harry, Suzanne, Peter, Travis, and Hayden, in hopes that you will always enjoy the ocean and its creatures.

—Lexington, MA
June 1999

Contents

The Compleat Crab and Lobster Book

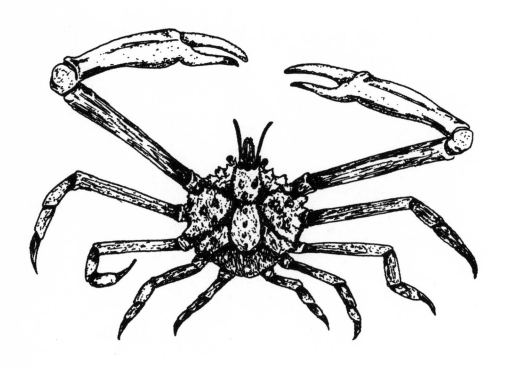

Introduction

WHEN I FINISHED WRITING *The Compleat Clammer*, now also being republished in a new and revised edition, I sensed that my work had just begun. To interact with the sea and to write about that interaction makes me feel doubly fortunate. Our ability to relate successfully to the sea, and to gain sustenance from it, must be protected. It also must be celebrated. The more we know about the food we take from the sea, the more we understand our own place in the natural world. I hope this book will enrich every seafood lover's appreciation of crabs and lobsters, whether boiling a lobster or making a Bayou crab casserole.

There is an unending human fascination with natural curiosities, whether noted in the world of "Ripley's Believe It or Not" or the "mysteries" and the "secrets" of nature, particularly of the ocean, since it covers some three-fourths of the earth's surface. P. T. Barnum, O. C. Marsh, and many others in the early twentieth century packed people into sideshows and museums to see such natural and yet new or rare creatures. And although we have come to understand that there is nothing freakish about the natural world, it is equally true that there is much we still have to learn. We seem to have revealed an unbroken and perhaps not fully understood need to be entertained, not simply informed, when we interact with our environment. And it is with at least a nod to this tradition that I try to offer not only the facts but also some curiosities about crabs and lobsters, as well as a few other crustaceans like crayfish and shrimp, that hopefully move my text toward a combination of information and entertainment. In short, this book is intended for both pleasure and reference, perhaps in accord with the Chinese proverb, "A book is like a garden carried in the pocket." And throughout, I urge you to respect the sea, to treat the ocean as the partner it must continue to be.

11

From a surimono *by Toyohiro*
The Ebi Takara-bune

1
Crabs and Lobsters 101

CRABS AND LOBSTERS. The very words evoke seemingly contradictory pictures that both frighten us and make our mouths water. Consider the crab. Everyone knows the crab is mean spirited, snappy, ugly, feisty, pugnacious, and brazenly unintimidated by man. For hundreds of years we have called nasty people "crabs." How common it is to find someone like Shakespeare writing, in *The Tempest*, "O she is ten times more gentle, than her father's crabbed" (III.1.8), or Thomas Carlyle following suit in his *French Revolution*, noting, ". . . his father, the harshest of old crabbed men." The human body, if bent or crooked, is said to be "crabbed," as is handwriting that is difficult to read. Then there are crab apples, those sour, bitter things—and it gets worse. The maligning associated with the word *crab* reminds me of how Loren Eisley summarized all the negatives associated with the word *left* in contrast to the word *right* when he said, "Well, no one ever created a 'bill of lefts'!"

There is crabgrass, which we try, usually unsuccessfully, to destroy. There is the phrase *catching a crab*, which means pulling a bad stroke in a crew race. In the 1940s, a freshman in any southern black college was called a "crab" by upperclassmen (Clarence Major, *Juba to Jive, A Dictionary of African-American Slang*). If you are "crab faced," you are definitely undesirable company. Crab Key was the island retreat of the darkly villainous Dr. No, James Bond's antagonist. There are crab lice, about which no more needs to be said. And above all, in the zodiac is the great crab cluster known unattractively as Cancer, our nemesis. The word *cancroid,* or crablike, not only describes certain creepy spiders but, in pathology, means "resembling cancer"; something can be of a cancerous or cancroid nature (from the Latin word *cancer,* meaning "crab"). And the negatives associated with crabs are common to cultures and traditions around the world. This is no western hang-up. Crab bashing has been popular for centuries.

Like a lot of other people all over the world, I *like* crabs, especially the wonderful Atlantic blue crab that is our primary interest. Crabs are a feisty and game quarry, filled with courage. The crab is beautiful in spirit, with the male protectively cradling the female in her vulnerable molted state. (I should also note that the female shows no such tenderness toward the vulnerable male, who in his weak-shelled state hides and hopes a hungry female won't come by and devour him.) Crabs have had a few good associations, ranging from occasional beliefs that they bring good luck to serving as symbols of speed (see "Slow-Flying Crabs" on p. 135). More often than not, though, we find people telling others to "crab it," meaning to back out, get lost. The negatives outweigh the positives.

Yet crabs are at the heart of some of the best cuisine in the world. Crab salad sandwiches, crab-stuffed tomatoes and avocados, crab cakes, crab quiche, crabs in spaghetti sauce, sautéed soft-shell crabs, crab bisque—I have included an entire chapter on crab cuisine and could easily have written a book on that subject alone.

While there are many kinds of crabs, the one of primary interest to us is the familiar Atlantic blue crab (*Callinectes sapidus*). This much-sought and long-prized creature lives principally along the Atlantic coast, ranging from Nova Scotia to Cape Cod, down around Florida to the Gulf of Mexico (it is also found in Bermuda and in a range from the West Indies to Uruguay). It is particularly abundant in the Chesapeake Bay, the "queen of the estuaries," whose very name has become synonymous with crab cuisine and whose crab fishermen have been exceedingly well presented in William Warner's wonderful classic, a must read for anyone interested in crabbing, *Beautiful Swimmers* (1976). The blue crab's name derives from the striking blue color on the male's claw, and more than one recreational crabber has felt his heart jump at the sight of that striking color peeking through some grasses in tidewater estuary.

One of the distinct pleasures of learning about crabs and crabbing is becoming familiar with a rich and wonderful language. Have a try at translating this paragraph:

Well, I had some luck with hard-shells. There were lots of Jimmys around and a few sooks; didn't find too many peelers or doublers—but there was one buck and rider over in the corner there. I picked up several busters and will be keeping them only a few days I suspect as I'd say they're ripe and will go any day. And soon the sallys will be getting it on.

Need help? The male blue crab is known as a "Jimmy" and the female as a "Sally" in her first summer, and then as a "sook." When the male and female are clasped together during the act of coupling, during the female's final molting stage (timed to coincide with reaching sexual maturity; see p. 20) as she waits for her new shell to harden, they are almost affectionately referred to as "doublers." Another name for them is "buck and rider." The blue crab is taken both when its shell is hard and when it is soft (the process of molting a shell and having a new one harden will be described shortly). Whether you order a soft-shell crab or a hard-shell, you are getting the exact same crab. (Note that the lobster is *not* good eating when its shell is soft, as its meat is overly filled with water and has, consequently, a mushy quality.) The soft-shell crab is called a "peeler" during the typical three-day duration it takes for its new shell to harden. A "buster" is a hard-shell crab that is close to busting out of its shell. Experienced crabbers can spot busters very easily, and often take them and keep them live in a tank of circulating salt water. When the busters bust, the fishermen have wonderful soft-shell crabs on their hands. When a male has shed its shell, it is sought out by females to be eaten, and sometimes such males are used as bait in "Jimmy potting" as a way of bringing the women in!

Understanding the life cycle of crabs, their patterns of behavior, and their basic mode of existence makes you a more knowledgeable hunter and a more appreciative adversary. The same holds true for lobsters, but let's begin with crabs.

The Biology of Crabs

The blue crab is one of the "true crabs" and, like the lobster, belongs to the Crustacea class, an extremely prolific and long-enduring group of marine invertebrates. As crustaceans, crabs are part of a larger group of creatures known as the arthropods (from the Greek words *arthron*, meaning "joint," and *podos* or *pous*, meaning "foot"). Crabs, like lobsters, are thus in the Arthropoda phylum, the Crustacea class, the Malacostraca subclass (true crabs), the Decapoda order (meaning "ten appendages"); they then have a family, a genus, and a species. Thus we would classify the blue crab in the following way:

Phylum Arthropoda
  Class Crustacea
    Subclass Malacostraca
      Order Decapoda
        Family Portunidae
          Genus *Callinectes*
            Species *sapidus*

All arthropods are joint-footed creatures, animals with many appendages, and all are also invertebrates (lacking a backbone). All of the creatures that come quickly to mind as having lots and lots of appendages—like spiders, centipedes, scorpions, and of course lobsters—are arthropods.

The blue crab's smooth carapace, or broad-back shell, is typically two to two and a half times longer than it is wide and is distinguished by its two sharp spines (points) on opposite ends of the length of the carapace. These sharp points, in fact, distinguish it from other species of crabs. There are eight short spines on each side running along the front edge between the pointed end spines and the eyes. The eyes are attached to collapsible stalks, set in recessed pockets, and between them we find four teeth and one little spine beneath them. The chelae, or big claws, are out in front, of slightly unequal size, followed by three pairs of smaller feet and a final pair of walking legs that have adapted into a flattened-out, paddle-shaped form. Actually, though the crab's paddle-shaped final set of limbs is advantageous in swimming, it is *disadvantageous* as well "in that the outline of the new exoskeleton in the thin paddle allows identification of premolt crabs," which are of course then caught and kept in

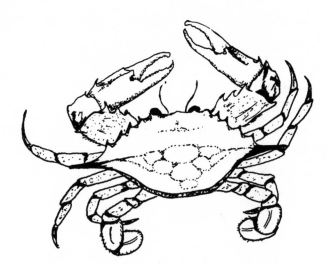

The Blue Crab, Callinectes Sapidus

cypresswood floats until they molt and are sold as soft-shell crabs (*McGraw-Hill Encyclopedia of Science and Technology,* p. 708). These five sets of symmetrical limbs add up to ten, giving us a deca-pod! Since the final pair of legs have become modified for swimming, they can't hurt you, and thus you can pick up a blue crab either by the paddles themselves (they can, however, break off) or, ideally, right between them, or in the middle of its back where the claws can't get you.

The blue crab is typically 5–7 inches across the carapace (you measure from lateral spine tip to spine tip, that is, straight across the back). The upper surface of the body is dark green, a mossy shade of deep olive; the underbody is a sort of eggshell or slightly yellowish white. The body is flattened out with the upper side slightly convex, with upper bumpy ins and outs being quite typical. The male crab is easily detected by the straight, narrow, pointed apron on his abdomen—as opposed to the broad V-shaped one of the female, which swells out when mature; the abdomen of the female spreads all the way across and becomes so filled with eggs that at times it points out from the carapace at a sharp angle. The creamy color of the underside of the crab, with a hint of pink and yellow, combined with the green back, leads some people to ask why it is called the blue crab—the answer comes from the bright blue color found on the male's front large claws (the *female's* claws are red).

The most important aspects of the crab for our purposes are its life cycle and its *lifestyle*. Usually in the late spring the female blue crab will develop a huge mass of eggs, as many as two million. She is known as a "sponge" in this phase (a female lobster at this point is referred to as a "berried" lobster, suggesting the fruit-bearing moment she is in), and it is usually against the law to keep her, for obvious ecological reasons (which is why, with apologies to old Charleston, South Carolina, I purposely omit "she-crab soup"; see p. 87).

Underside of a Crab

 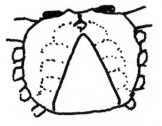 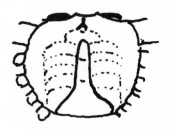

Mature Female   *Immature Female*   *Male*

When the eggs hatch they are microscopic larvae, and, as part of the planktonic food chain, most are eaten. Those that survive, however, will experience the molting or shell-shedding process some twenty to thirty times in a lifetime. The crab actually grows a new shell underneath its old shell, then breaks out of the old shell by slipping out through the side. When they are very tiny, crabs molt every three to five days, and as they grow the intervals of time get longer between each molting, with twenty- to fifty-day intervals being common. As crabs get larger, the process takes longer—as much as three hours of active work when mature. When the female is getting close to having her final molt, the male crab or Jimmy finds her and carries her around for a few days. She prepares for having the male copulate with her as her apron expands from a V-shaped to a more circular, fuller egg-carrying shape. The male and the female are then locked in copulation for from six to twelve hours; for the female, this mating takes place only once. As William Warner notes, "For her it is a once-in-a-lifetime experience. Its duration is heroic, however." The male then goes off, but not without first protecting her for several days as her shell hardens ("Such consideration is not known to exist among many other species of crab," Warner notes), and eventually finds another female who needs his protection, and his seed! That the male protects the female in her final molt and stays with her after copulation is one of nature's more romantic stories. That the male knows instinctively when the female is nearing her final molt is also something of a miracle. The male generally gets up on his legs as high as he can to indicate his courtship approach, and the female generally rocks from side to side, sometimes turning around and backing rather unsubtly toward the male.

Incidentally, while a soft-shell crab is delicious (see p. 77), eating one whose shell has *just* begun to harden is to be avoided because, in its soft-shell state, the crab has not been able to hunt and eat in a regular way; its body is depleted and thus its meat is not as tasty.

During the winter months the crabs migrate to deeper waters, but when spring comes and the water becomes warmer, they head inland and work their way into estuaries, rivers, tidal flats, and virtually all kinds of relatively shallow (20 feet or so) waters where there is a good supply of food. Their eyes come up out of their sockets on stalks so they can see efficiently (crabs, unlike lobsters, are known for outstanding vision, which you will realize the first time you look at one looking back at you in the eye as you are trying to keep it on your handline!), and they crawl, swim, burrow, and generally go about their business of scavenging for food, especially liking dead animal matter of virtually any kind. They swim sideways by using the legs on one side to push while the legs on the other side pull (much like our own side-stroke when swimming). Like other common swimming crabs, such as the lady crab and the green crab, the blue crab is an intelligent hunter, searching for food around dock pilings or other places where people may have thrown away anything from scallop shells to old bait to fish heads.

As the months go by, the crabs feed and grow, and when they molt, they increase their size typically by as much as a third, with several major molts in the summer months. By July and August, we have good-sized crabs to capture, and since a great deal of mating occurs in the late summer, big crabs often come into very shallow areas looking for protective grasses. Poling through saltwater marshes and estuaries will generally bring you up on lots of crabs.

The key, of course, is to be able to see them. On Shelter Island, New York, we have had trouble in recent years with "brown tide." This problem, the subject of massive research, is essentially an unmitigated buildup of algae that prevents sunlight from reaching the eelgrass, thereby reducing, in turn, both the eelgrass and the scallops. Years ago, you could look straight down some 8–10 feet into Coeckles Harbor and see everything on the bottom as clear as if looking through air. Things will hopefully get better in the next few years, especially with closer monitoring of sewage runoff capacity (excess makes the water warmer and the algae flourish). Scallops bring more crabs, but even assuming that there are still many crabs around, they are harder to see and thus harder to catch by scapping from a boat (see p. 48). The same goes for "firelighting" or night crabbing (see p. 59), with murkier waters making the process more difficult. The relationship between the prevalence of the scallop and that of the blue crab should not be underestimated. For example, when scallops were at their height several years ago, the late Captain Frank Beckwith would typically bring up five to seven good-sized crabs in his scallop dragnet every time.

In *The Compleat Clammer* I noted that much scientific research is being done on clams. The same holds true for the blue crab. Researchers have focused particularly on the Chesapeake Bay, where it is estimated, for example, that some 48 percent of the total of East and Gulf Coast hard crab landings took place in 1985.* Scientists are less interested in the Virginia and Maryland watermen than they are in the blue crab's predators, pollutants, plants and other animals with symbiotic relationships to the blue crab, parasites, diseases, salinity, temperatures, oxygen, heavy metals, and various environmental issues. As has been noted by various scientists who study the Chesapeake Bay, where the water quality has been deteriorating from industrial pollutants, it is for-

---

*See discussions of research in the various proceedings of the Philadelphia 1986 conference on "Chesapeake Bay Fisheries and Contaminant Problems."

tunate that the blue crab's earliest life is in fact spent outside of the bay rather than in it! It is also fortunate that the research has been accelerating in recent years and that the environmental and economic importance of the blue crab is being carefully highlighted by scientific findings.

Knowing as much as you can about crabs and their cycle puts you ahead in your quest to catch them, and even if you buy all of your crabs (I buy soft-shell crabs, to be honest, more often than I catch them), it is fun to understand them. You need to check regulations carefully in the area where you go. (This point will be made a number of times throughout the book, and detailed current directions are included in the appendix.) Three inches is the usual legal size for peelers, 3½ inches for soft-shells. Since crabs that are hatched in June will take thirteen or fourteen months to reach their full size, it is important not to take them too small. Given a typical life span of about three years for the blue crab, and the number of molts they experience (estimates are generally a total of eighteen to twenty for females and twenty-one to twenty-three for males, not that the difference matters significantly), we need to recognize that all of this takes time—we need to respect the process and tie in to it, not foul it up.

Blue crabs usually spend some of the winter buried in the mud and in deeper water (as deep as 120 feet), but as the spring approaches and the water grows warmer, they migrate into shallower warmer water. Typically crabs born the previous year are now several inches long and have not experienced a molting during the winter dormancy; thus they are too small to catch. As the summer progresses they molt a number of times, growing proportionately longer each time and also being bolder about moving toward fresher water—all crabs like the general estuarine habitat, where salt water and fresh water merge, as in the Chesapeake Bay.

When the crabs have moved into the warmer, shallower water, both commercial and recreational crabbing begin to get fully under way. The crabs are of different ages and have arrived for three purposes—feeding, molting, and reproducing.

In the early fall the fertilized females will head for deeper water, and shortly the males will follow, though not to be with the females. (Considerable dredging for dormant crabs takes place in the late fall and winter.) When spring approaches, the now two-year-old male will sometimes come back in or sometimes simply die. The female will come in and drop her eggs in the warmer water needed by the young, and then she typically will die, although sometimes she goes through several more cycles of reproduction.

The blue crab typically reaches sexually maturity in thirteen months and breeds during July and August. The female has about 1.75 million eggs. When she comes in from the deeper waters the massive egg sponge under her abdomen soon bursts and in about two weeks the eggs hatch into larvae that don't yet look like crabs. After several molts they become megalops, which in turn molt into tiny crabs, which then experience successive molts.

It is interesting to note increasing interest in the molting of crabs. There is, it turns out, gold in them thar shells. Alaskan seafood packagers once dumped so many crab shells into Kodiak Harbor that an enormous mess was being made. It may be possible for the ocean to deal fairly easily with the shells that the crabs throw away naturally, but when *man* enters the situation and dumps tons of crab shells in one place, the scenario changes. In this case, however, researchers discovered that the crab shells are a wonderful source of a natural polymer called chitin (pronounced kite-in), which is now being used in a variety of ways— from cleansing polluted waters and enhancing crop yields to treating burns and doubling as a soluble surgical suture. The

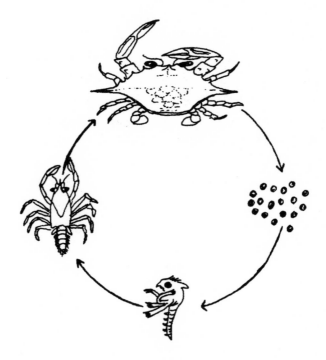

Life Cycle of a Crab

result is that there is now a large and growing chitin-recovery industry in the United States and Japan. All of which reminds us yet again of our profound ignorance about the ocean and its wonders. (And having visited a canning operation in Ketchican, Alaska, in 1997, I can assure you that chitin recovery is not an activity we want to curtail!)

Crabbing rewards a combination of skill, patience, aggression, and charisma. This last is necessary because the crab, at one point or another as it eats the chicken neck or fish head on your line while you pull it in, is going to see you. And at that point nothing short of pure charm will keep it on. Drawing a crab line in is like flying a kite in that you must concentrate and communicate with the tension in the line.

Some of the best and happiest crabbing I have done has been at Pawleys Island in South Carolina. I would go out red snapper fishing in the gulf one day, usually out of Murrell's Inlet, then use the fish heads for crab bait the next day. Across from the small cottage I rented for my family, sun-bleached gray docks jutted out into the tidal creek. From these docks we would set out our hand-lines and consistently pull in some good-sized crabs. The setting was beautiful, and we would often see a clapper rail, a few egrets and herons, and quietly keep pulling the crabs in. My then-small daughters would enjoy it for about a half an hour, then they would begin making expressions to indicate that it was time for a faster-paced activity.

That crabs are crustaceans gives them an extraordinarily rich phylogeny; they are part of a class with a geologic history of 350 million years! Some species are found 12,000 feet high in the water of melted snow, and others are found 6 miles deep in the sea's darkest holes. However, our female blue crabs tend to migrate into water in the winter that is only 20–30 feet deep. The males stay around longer than the females, and even make an effort to endure in the deeper holes around their usual haunts—until the water temperature drops to around 50 degrees, and then they too head farther out to greater depths.

The Biology of Lobsters

Lobsters are also malacostracans or higher crustaceans. Their class includes the large and generally very familiar creatures like crabs, shrimp, and crayfish, and all in their order have essentially the same plan: a thorax that has eight segments and an abdomen that has seven (sometimes six if the last two have become fused, as often occurs); the female has an oviduct on the sixth thoracic segment, and the male has his counterpart genital duct on the eighth thoracic segment.

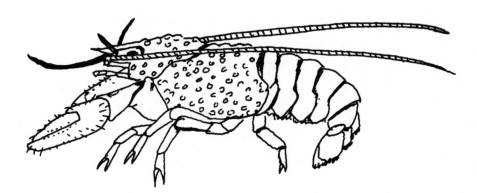

Crayfish

Lobsters are in the Decapoda order, as are crabs; the langouste or spiny lobsters are in the section Palinura; freshwater crayfish and the lobsters we are interested in are in the section Astacura, in the family Homaridae. *Homarus americanus*, the American lobster, is the one we all generally catch and buy and enjoy cracking open. There are other lobsters you may hear about from time to time. One is the European lobster, only about half the size of its American counterpart. Another is the even smaller South African cape lobster, which only is about 4 or 5 inches long.

Here is how we classify our favorite lobster:

Phylum Arthropoda
Class Crustacea
Subclass Malacostraca
Order Decapoda
Family Nephropidae
Genus *Homarus*
Species *americanus*

Like such other decapods as crabs, shrimp, and crayfish, lobsters have their thoracic segments "fused with those of the head to form the cephalothorax, which is covered by the carapace."* In lobsters the carapace is cylindrical, whereas in the blue crab it is flattened out. While lobsters have their head and thorax fused, crabs have much smaller abdomens. Like crabs, lobsters have eyes on stalks (I always think of them as periscopes).

From the days when colonists first stepped ashore in New England, lobsters have caught the fancy of Americans. The arriving settlers soon discovered that lobsters were delicious, but it is also the case that because lobsters were so abundant, the settlers sometimes planted them with their corn as fertilizer and caught and used so many that the American lobster has never been as plentiful since—and the steadily rising prices now indicate scarcity. Research has revealed that back in 1630, for example, anybody could catch and eat all the lobsters he wanted, with many weighing over 25 pounds.

The decrease in the supply of American lobsters was propelled by the popularity of canned lobster in the late nineteenth century. More canned lobster than live lobster was being sold out of Maine in the 1880s. Some twenty-three canneries by that time were busily processing and shipping some 2 *million* pounds of lobster meat annually—"and even then, business was thought to be in decline, having peaked in landings and profitability ten years before. By the 1870s, processors were picking the meat of twenty or thirty half-pound lobsters to fill

---

*R. Headstrom, *All About Lobsters, Crabs, Shrimps and their Relatives*, N.Y., p. 29. An excellent, very detailed guide to the anatomy and physiology of lobster and crabs.

a one-pound can."* It is not coincidental that as lobsters of only a ½ pound were being torn open, the new law against keeping berried female was passed, in 1872. But let's get back to biology.

The decapods divide into three groups, depending on the nature of their tails. The Macrura—including the lobsters, shrimp, and crayfish—are all large tailed, whereas the Anomura have oddly shaped tails (the hermit crabs and the mole crab are good examples), and the Brachyura, like the true crabs (our blue crab among them), are short tailed. The so-called tail of the crab is actually the abdomen, that part of the body that has been folded under behind the stomach.

Crayfish, or *ecrevisse* as the French call them, closely resemble lobsters, but while they are of the same order, they live in fresh water. Their similarity to lobsters is often noted, and there is even an Australian crayfish species known as the "Murray River lobster." In North America alone there are some 250 species and subspecies of crayfish. In Louisiana, which accounts for about 90 percent of the commercially cultivated crayfish in this country, there are twenty-nine species. There are different types of crayfish all over the world. They are indigenous on every continent except Africa and Antarctica. They like to burrow under rocks during the day and seek food at night. The two principal families of crayfish are the Astacidae (of the Northern Hemisphere) and the Parastacidae (of the Southern Hemisphere). In Germany they have the wonderful name *Steinkrebs*. Given their freshwater environment, I have decided not to treat them at length in this book, although I must note that there are some fantastic ways to prepare them.

---

*From Jason Stone's very interesting article on lobsters and the history of lobstering, which appeared in announcing the opening of the Maine Maritime Museum's permanent exhibit "Lobstering on the Maine Coast" in Bath, Maine. "Homage to the Lobster," *Down East*, Vol. 32, No. 11, June 1986.

Hermit Crab   Ghost Crab

All creatures of the sea live in what are referred to as "zones." The highest is known as the "splash zone" (or "supralittoral zone") because creatures living here are literally kept alive simply by receiving some light splashes of the ocean water. There are several kinds of shore crabs and a rock louse that spend most of their time out of the water. In the "high-tide zone" we discover creatures that feed only as the high tide brings food to them; otherwise they are out of water. Certain shore crabs, some limpets, and many barnacles are found here. In her classic book *The Edge of the Sea*, Rachel Carson describes in a wonderful way the manner in which ghost crabs (my family and I studied them daily on the wide coastal beaches of Pawleys Island), for example, come scurrying down from the high, dry sandy area of the beach to the edge of the water to get wet, then scurry back up farther on the land. "At intervals during each day they must go down to the water line to wet their gills, accomplishing their purpose with the least possible contact with the sea. Instead of wading directly into the water, they take up a position a little above the place where, at the moment, most of the waves are breaking on the beach. They stand sideways to the water, gripping the sand with the legs on the landward side. Human bathers know that in any surf an occasional wave will tower higher than the others and run further up the beach. The crabs wait, as if they also know this, and after such a wave has washed over them, they return to the upper beach."* Incidentally, the ghost crab (*Ocypode quadrata*) is so named because it blends so perfectly with the sand that it is almost indiscernible; it is also very fast moving.

In the "middle-tide zone" (or "midlittoral zone") you find a number of creatures, like certain mussels and some tiny crabs, that live on rocky surfaces washed by the ocean but remain much of the time out in the open air. In the "low-tide zone" (infralittoral zone") you find the shellfish, the oysters and clams, as well as starfish, chitons, some sea anemones, and so forth. These low-tide creatures benefit from the regular changing of the tide but are not dependent on being in the water all of the time. Just the opposite is true of lobsters, which live, along with many kinds of fish, in the "pelagic zone," the huge area that covers all of the surfaces and subsurfaces of the ocean. This heavily populated world of life, teeming with eels and fish and our favorite largest crustacean, is distanced only by the final or "abyssal zone" that begins over 600 feet deep, far from the reach of light, and that is inhabited by countless creatures that are still being regularly discovered. In 1981, for example, some shrimplike crustaceans known as amphipods were recovered for the first time live from

---

*Rachel Carson, *The Edge of the Sea*, N.Y., 1955, p. 138.

the depth of about 6 miles—the very deepest region of the ocean yet known, the so-called Challenger Deep in the Mariana Trench. The animals were brought up from the bottom—the pressure is enormous and the water 2 degrees Celsius—in pressurized traps by researchers working out of the Scripps Institute of Oceanography in La Jolla, California (reported in *Sea Technology*, February 1981).

There are four families of lobsters: "true lobsters" (Homaridae); spiny lobsters (Palinuridae); slipper lobsters, also known as Spanish lobsters (Scyllaridae); and deep-sea lobsters (Polychelidae). The lobster of the East Coast is a true lobster known, once again, as the species *Homarus americanus*, generally simply called the American or Northern lobster. It ranges from North Carolina and Virginia north to Labrador, going always into deeper water during the fall and then into shallower water in the summer (though some, it has been determined, stay in somewhat shallower water year-round). It travels from shoreline to the Continental Shelf.

What most distinguishes the American lobster are its huge chelae, or pincer-claws, on the ends of the front set of walking feet; these claws make up between one-fourth and one-half the weight of a lobster. The larger of these two claws is used to crush hard bivalves and snails, while the smaller "cutter" claw tears apart both meat and plants as it feeds. There are very small claws on the next two pairs, and little hooks on the final ones. The final pair of legs have not been modified into swimming paddles, as with the blue crab, but the lobster does have swimmerets (the small flattened appendages along the tail); the lobster relies on hard snapping flicks of its powerful tail to swim backward, and thus uses all ten of its feet for walking. It creeps most of the time, crawling around on rocky bottoms in the deep ocean and in bays, and hiding underneath rocks and in crevices. (Some believe that

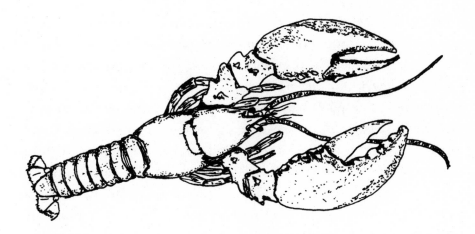

Lobster

its eyesight is not particularly good and that it half bumps into what it eats as it wanders around looking for decaying and dead matter—its scavenger personality is very much in concert with that of the crab.) The lobster's tail is well engineered, with the appendages on its next-to-last body segment flattened out to help create a kind of paddle. The lobster eats fish, snails, sea urchins, and starfish; it can use its large claw to dig out a clam (its antennae serve as detectors) and crush the clam's shell to eat it. (As I frequently observe in *The Compleat Clammer*, there is a great deal of competition as we hunt for clams!)

The female lobster's eggs are attached to her abdominal legs with a kind of glue, and when the eggs hatch the larval lobsters, called zoeae, continue to stick to the mother for a period of time. Lobsters go through a series of moltings—as crabs do—in order to grow, each time developing a new shell before bursting out of the old one. Given lobsters' larger size and longer life (they can be fifty years old and have been captured in the 45- to 50-pound range), the molting process is more cumbersome and takes longer, and is less frequent as the years progress. Here is an excellent scientific description from Augusta Foote Arnold's well-known guidebook, first published in the beginning of the twentieth century, *The Sea-Beach at Ebb-Tide*: "The lobster molts eight times the first year, five times the second, and three times the third year, after which the male molts twice and the female once a year. It retires to some secluded spot for this operation, which is attended with many dangers. The back splits open longitudinally and the animal slowly withdraws, leaving the shell complete. In preparation for molting, the lime around the contracted joints of the chelae is absorbed, so that the soft flesh can pass through." Unlike crabs, which have a relatively short life, lobsters live a very long time. The females can have successive couplings and egg hatchings, unlike the she-crab, which has the experience only once. It seems possible that the female lobster sometimes molts only every other year (see G. E. MacGintie and N. MacGintie, *Natural History of Marine Animals*. Indeed, the exact number of molts is subject to ongoing analysis; the one certain thing is that by the time a lobster is some 10 inches long, it has molted about twenty-five times and is about five years old.

The first mating of the lobster occurs when the female is four or five years old. The lobster lays her eggs in the summer months, mostly in July and August, releasing the eggs slowly over a period of several weeks. A very unusual fact characterizes the fertilization process: The male lobster releases his sperm onto the female (unlike crabs, lobsters copulate in a face-to-face embrace), usually right after she has molted, and she carries it around with her in pockets on her underside, then uses the sperm to fertilize the eggs as she lays them. The sperm deposited by the male lobster is usable for several months, though generally gets used

sooner rather than later. Still, it is one of nature's more ingenious plans. The hatching of the eggs usually lasts for about a
week, following an incubation period of ten or eleven months. A
10-inch lobster typically has about ten thousand eggs; smaller
ones have fewer and larger ones have more, with a high of
around a hundred thousand (a far cry from the two million eggs
a female blue crab may hatch, but then she only gets to do it
once!). The American lobster spawns once every other year,
which is reasonable given the long incubation period—and also
explains the importance of not taking berried lobsters, particularly because some 90 percent of lobsters caught and kept are
just barely the legal size. In most states you are required to
gauge, or measure, a lobster as you catch it and before putting it
with your catch. Thus if caught with an undersized lobster you
cannot claim in defense that you have not gauged it yet.

People have long worried about having a sufficient supply of
lobsters, way before the canning "crisis" of the 1880s. Even by
the end of the eighteenth century, cities like Boston and New
York were hungry for all the lobster they could get. Since lobsters
had to be transported live, "well smacks," or small sailing vessels
with circulating saltwater tanks aboard, were developed and common along the coasts of New England by the 1820s. There does
not, in fact, seem to be a time when the demand for lobster has
not been great and anxiety about the supply high. Luckily lobsters, like other marine animals, vastly overproduce. We are not
likely to run out of lobsters, any more than we are likely to run
out of crabs, but we must continue to work with those who manage our environment, and never at cross-purposes. We all hope
that each morning boats with lobstermen will continue to set out
for the rocky shoals.

In a sense many pelagic creatures, not just lobsters, are scav-
engers, cruising around to see what they can find. Lobsters do not

scavenge indiscriminately. True, they eat a good amount of "junk food," but so do many creatures, including man. Lobsters, like crabs, also eat one another (preying cannibalistically on their younger, smaller relatives), they go for fish, and, alas, they dig for clams. I like to think of lobsters as what might be called "entrepreneurial" eaters, and perhaps all of this variety on their part is at the heart of their own delicious taste. They certainly have been led into one of the widest of all imaginable diets! Given the way lobsters migrate into water up to some 600 feet deep in the fall, and in the spring return to waters as shallow as 6 feet, they need to eat what they encounter at an enormous variety of depths. You can see why they cannot get hung up on one particular snack! Lobsters clearly enjoy live food like mollusks and fish, and, of course, even a little salad (vegetation) on the side.

Lobsters and Crabs in Art

Perhaps because lobsters have not only long antennae (they can reach all the way behind them to feel what is there if they want to back up!) but also long life, they have been much celebrated in Japanese culture and art. Known as the *ebi* and resembling the spiny lobster more than the American, the lobster is used as a symbol of longevity and also to decorate announcements of special activities. Its bright red color is highlighted on many congratulatory cards and New Year decorations. Known as *surimono*, or "ceremonial cards," these lobster-bearing illustrations are very engaging, and well described and exemplified in Katherine M. Ball's large, authoritative book *Decorative Motives of Oriental Art*. Lobsters are sometimes used to symbolize the hulls of treasure-bearing ships. Sometimes the *surimono* have a message of this not entirely flattering or comforting sort, illustrating the point of longevity: "May you live until your back humps like the lobster." Although not as common in the traditions of China, in art the lobster appears as a craft being sailed by one of the great Taoists, Hsiang Tzu.

In China it is the crab that receives the most attention. And of course the crab is represented in the zodiac, where in the sign of Cancer it symbolizes the retrograde movement of the sun after it has crossed the summer solstice and is taking a backward course—clearly in keeping with what we know about crabs. Indeed, this sideways movement captivated the Chinese; "it was this sidewise movement that led the Orientals to designate the European penmanship as 'crab-writing' because it is done horizontally, while Chinese ideographs are always written in vertical columns" (Ball, p. 183). Because the crab goes off and disappears during the winter months and then returns, the Chinese considered it a good symbol for the sleep of death between reincarnations; thus in the Himalayas and other remote parts of China, sacred crabs are kept in vessels in front of the temples.

There are various other superstitions surrounding crabs and lobsters that appear in the arts of the Orient, but we also know that the ability to restore lost claws has particularly struck many cultures as a magical sort of power. In Egypt the sign of Cancer is represented by the scarab, an emblem of immortality. It is logical as a symbol in a way that some symbols are not, and surely the ability of crabs and lobsters to replace lost appendages (see p. 142) is one of nature's more remarkable inventions that man envies. In any case, crabs in Japanese art, while not as numerous, have their own sets of legends, and in both China and Japan we can find crabs and lobsters in virtually all media, such as textiles, ivory, lacquer, porcelain, and—above all in attractiveness—the beautifully designed bronze crabs (which in replication have been marketed increasingly as ashtrays, with the backs lifting up).

Lobsters and Crabs: Legends and Literature

As noted earlier, lobsters and particularly crabs are not always revered. On the back of a crab there is a certain imprint that the Japanese believe represents the Heike, a group of defeated warriors who, after losing a battle in the twelfth century against the Genji family, committed mass suicide by heaving themselves into the sea—where, legend has it, they were turned into crabs with their faces becoming those imprints on the crabs' backs. The Siamese believe that giant crabs are responsible for their ships being sunk. In many European waters, crabs are considered great villains, especially perhaps the Chinese mitten crab, which is known to undermine and do structural damage to dikes, as in the flooding of the Netherlands in 1953. And so it goes, praise and blame. Even Barclay writing in 1509 in his *Shyp of Folys* noted, "One crab blames another for her backwater pace, And yet the blamer can none other do" (1.78). And in Shakespeare's *Hamlet* we find the following witticism: "You your selfe Sir, should be old as I am, if like a Crab you could go backward" (II,ii,205). It was Aristophanes who apparently coined the expression, incidentally, that "you cannot teach a crab to walk straight" (*Peace,* 1.1083). Whether positively worshiped for longevity and regeneration power or lampooned for being backward and moving in odd ways generally, crabs and lobsters emerge in art and literature in surprising places.

As just one humorous example consider the following, by the early-nineteenth-century Russian writer Ivan Krylov. He wrote a fable incorporating rather wryly the crab's way of traveling; in the tale a crab, a swan, and a pike set out together to pull a wagon:

It was not that their load was difficult to move,
But upward strained the swan, toward skies above,
The crab kept stepping back, the pike was for the pond.
And which was right or wrong, I neither know nor care.
I only know the wagon's still there.

(As included in A. S. Mercatanta, *Zoo of the Gods: Animals in Myth, Legend, and Fable*).

Some people have been done in by their enthusiasm for crabs or lobsters, such as the chef Vatel, who was in charge of preparing the grand feast given by the grande Conde to Louis XIV at Chantilly; he was, so legend has it, "told that the lobsters for the turbot sauce had not arrived, whereupon this chef of kitchen retired to his private room, and, leaning on his sword ran it through his body, unable to survive such a dire disgrace as serving up turbot without lobster sauce" (as told in E. C. Brewer, *Dictionary of Phrase and Fable*, London, 1902).

Let's move on to describing how to catch, cook, open, serve, and enjoy crabs and lobsters—in not one but many, many ways. For while we no longer take a hundred million lobsters out of the water annually, and while we no longer have unlimited supplies of crabs crawling onto our bait lines and into our traps, they are out there and ready to be caught and eaten. If it's true, as Erasmus and others have asserted, that *cancer leporem capit* ("the crab catches the hare," a variation on the tortoise and the hare), it is equally true that we catch the crab and the lobster! Anyway, it's time to take Chaucer's advice and "turn over the leef and ches another tale."

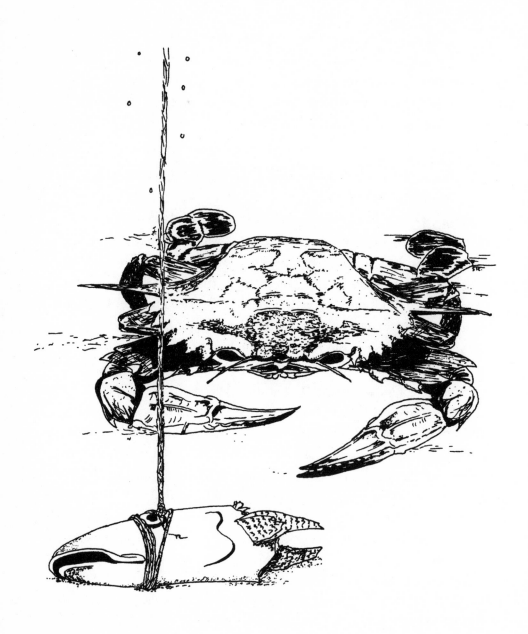

2

Catching the Feisty Blue Crab

❦

IMPORTANT NOTE: BEFORE SETTING out to catch crabs, and no matter what way of catching them you select, take the time to become familiar with the crabbing regulations that obtain in a particular location (I have included the names, addresses, and phone numbers of appropriate agencies in all U.S. coastal states in the appendix).

There are essentially a half-dozen ways of catching crabs, and certain variations on all of them: handlining; scapping (also known as "baitless crabbing"); trapping; trotlining; potting; and jacklighting or night crabbing. For the amateur recreational crabber, the first two are the most common and most easily mastered methods.

Six Ways to Catch a Crab

Handlining

Standing on a dock or a shoreline that leads to a good crabbing catch usually places you in a wonderful locale. One of my favorite spots, for example, is in the inlet that runs on the backside of Pawleys Island, South Carolina. Our whole family has enjoyed walking out onto a short weather-beaten gray dock armed with our handlines and nets, our bait and pails, and in an hour or so

Handlining

we have often caught all the crabs we could eat or give away. It's not that easy everywhere or every time, but the technique is always the same.

A handline is simply a long piece of strong white cotton or nylon cord that runs from your hand on one end to piece of bait that a crab can grab on to on the other. By standing on a dock, going off the side of a boat, working from a bulkhead or even a bridge, you can sink a piece of bait to the bottom, using some extra weights beyond the weight of the bait if the current so requires to keep the bait on the bottom, and find crabs as they move about with the tide. Their exploration of the murky estuaries will surely bring them to discover your bait.

Crabs like to scavenge for food. They will not eat just anything, however, so don't make the mistake of thinking that you can use as bait just any old garbage. Give them a little credit. Use crab bait that is known to work and easy to procure, like fish heads, pieces of fish, chicken necks, or other poultry parts, for best results. Chicken necks are particularly good because it is difficult for the crab to pull the flesh from the bone, and the crab will therefore cling tenaciously—which is what you want, since your goal is to pull the bait slowly and steadily toward you until you can see the crab.

Usually you will know from the weight and the resistance on your line that a crab has fastened itself onto the bait. Be careful: Don't just haul the bait all the way up, for the crab will let go if you do. Usually you will see a glint of claw or even an eye as the bait comes into view (generally between 12 and 18 inches under the surface, depending on the murkiness of the water), at which point you will need to be readying your net.

Be sure to tie your line carefully around the piece of bait (if you use extra weights to stay on the bottom, tie the bait slightly above the weights so the weights, not the bait, are in the mud). I like to tie the bait up quite well, as I have discovered that crabs see the string and seem not to care at all! There is nothing more vexing than to bring a crab in and see it leave your line with the bait.

A handline is usually tied around a piece of wood or a square so that it can easily be coiled up before and after you begin. I like to use a heavy fishing line, but any cotton or nylon twine will work well too. Fish heads are the bait I have used most, partly because they are free, saved from a catch or picked up at a fish market (they can be stuck in the freezer for a whole season and used as well; crabs are not very selective). Tie your line through the fish head's eyes or carefully through the mouth, wrap it a few times, and it should stay secure. Red snapper heads are great if you are in South Carolina, but any oily fish works well; bluefish heads are great in the mid-Atlantic range, and menhaden or tautog (blackfish) are also good and oily fleshed. Keeping some slack in the line, you gently toss the fish head out into the water and let it settle to the bottom; if you are in an inlet or an estuary where there is a strong current, use some lead weights tied close

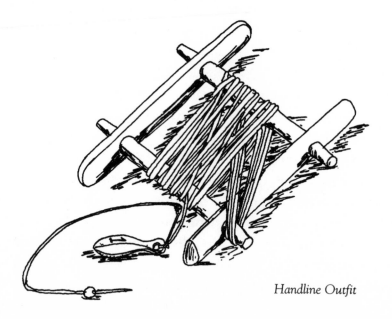

Handline Outfit

to the bait, as it is important that the bait stay right on the bottom. Crabs sometimes clasp on to the bait before it reaches the bottom, so you want to be feeling for that, but in general you will, after waiting for a minute or so, feel the handline begin to become taut. Pull (don't jerk) the line slowly, almost imperceptibly, toward you, and if there is more resistance or the bait seems heavier, you will know that you have a crab (or several, if you're lucky) engaged. Use a crab net, easily purchased at any marine hardware store or fishing station, ideally made of cotton.

Now comes the hard part.

Once a crab has fastened on to your bait, he or she is, we assume, extremely pleased. How ordinary the rest of the bottom of the bay must seem, compared to a big fresh piece of chicken or a bright head of a fish. This isn't just normal scavenger's fare. This fact works in your favor, because it means the crab does not really want to let go. Imagine putting a chocolate chip cookie in your mouth and not trying to eat it! Still, your job is to draw the line in steadily, without jerkiness or sudden movements, and to have your crab net extended and ready. Slow, steady pulling is the key to success, or in the words of an old Chinese proverb frequently quoted by my late mother-in-law, Mary Arny, "Softly, softly, catchee monkey!" With practice you can pull the line with one hand, or use a few fingers from the hand holding the net. Keep the net from throwing any shadow over the path of the handline, and remember that once the bait gets close to the surface of the water, the crab is going to let go. At first you may want to get a partner and work as a team, with one person working the handline and the other standing ready to scoop the net under the crab and the bait (be sure to scoop under both the crab and the bait; some people make the mistake of trying to net just the crab). Aluminum nets are light and practical. Nets of standard 6-foot length are best unless you have an exceptionally long reach to get to the water, in which case a longer-handled net is better, though harder to work with.

Crabs are very wary, and the moment they suspect foul play they will let go. It's not like fishing, where at least you have a hook in the fish. All you have is the crab's will to hang on, and you must play to this will in every way you can. Be quiet, and move slowly. One helpful trick is to tie a colored piece of string at several points along your handline so that you will know how much farther you have to tow the crab—with some practice you can scoop it before you see it, which means before it sees you and lets go.

Be patient. Some beginning crabbers believe that a blue crab will find the bait immediately. In fact, the crab *does* find your bait very fast, usually faster than a fish, for example. But it still takes some time, and you should test your line every so often before beginning to pull it in. I think it is best to have several hand-lines, so you can go from one to the other feeling for a tug. This tends to make you more patient and forces an interval of time before you check again to see if you have one. On the other hand, if you have a crab on each line you have to work on just one, knowing (and it is an irritating kind of knowledge) that another crab is getting away with murder as it eats the bait happily on the other line with no contest!

When you find you have a crab on your line, you may find yourself surprised by the strength behind the tugging. Remember that the crab's claws hold on sixty times more tightly than the human grip in relation to the body weight. This can be converted from a plus for the crab to a plus for you! That the crab is a scavenger works in your favor; on the other claw, you should remember that we all drop a hot potato.

I interpret all of this to mean that you must, when crabbing, think like a dissembler. Do some acting. You are trying to make it easy for your quarry to catch itself. A clam doesn't dig up toward you and a fish doesn't just go for a hook. When crabbing with a handline you must be very still and quiet. Anyone who bends over a dock edge and addresses the crab ("Come to Papa") is not performing like the Artful Dodger; to crab successfully you have to bring some street smarts out to the shore.

Many people who have tried handlining have made some of the following mistakes, so try to be on the watch. First, it is easy to forget that *your* end of the line is as important as the crab's. If you go to scoop up the crab and drop your line into the water, and miss the crab, you're out a handline and the crab can spend the next few hours happily separating the bait from the line. Tie your stick, or whatever you have your line wrapped on, to something else, like a dock piling, or even your foot. Just protect yourself from accidentally letting it all go. Second, you will need to empty the crab into your basket or pail carefully, because picking up a scurrying crab on a dock is difficult, and you can get badly clawed by a big pincer. If the crab does get loose try to place your foot (wearing sneakers or Docksiders) lightly on the back of the crab, and then pick it up carefully by one of the back flippers or at the rear of the carapace between them; that way pincers cannot reach your hand. Try to get your net into the water ahead of the crab. It is much better to pull the crab slowly into the path of the already positioned net than it is to make a mad scoop at the crab when it comes into sight. I like to get my net in the water before I start to pull at all; this can save valuable split seconds. It is also unwise to begin to pull in the crab the second you sense its presence. Let the crab enjoy its newly discovered supermeal and then, as it's fully engaged and feeling spoiled, begin to pull it in. Keep the angle of your handline low so that the crab's ascent is not too suddenly upward; it's more natural and less suspicious for it to travel on a graduated incline.

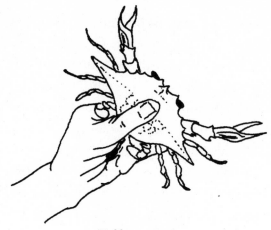

Holding a Crab

A crab net with a mesh of several inches if fine; if you use a net with too small a mesh, it is harder to disengage the crab. To dump a crab from a net, first try simply to turn it over into your pail with one quick movement. Usually only a few of its limbs will be hanging on. If it gets tangled up in the net, remember to grab it by the flippers and slowly work it out. If it holds on to the net with one or two pincers, flip it over the basket. If you shake the net lightly it will release its grip and drop into the basket. The sound of the clattering in the basket when a newly caught crab arrives is wonderful!

It's not cool to smoke anymore, but if you do, don't while crabbing. You want to be able to hold your line and carefully pull it in with one hand and be positioning your net with the other. Unless you have three hands, smoking while crabbing is as hindering as smoking while making love!

Scapping (Baitless Crabbing)

Believe it or not, you can catch crabs without any bait at all. This is known as scapping, or simply taking a crab net and carefully scooping crabs into it. It's not as easy as it sounds.

To scap for crabs you have to talk with locally knowledgeable people. These days you can't just wade into the water anywhere and hope to have any success. On Shelter Island, where I enjoy crabbing, I scap in several ways that are fairly typical. My favorite (and most successful) is to walk slowly into backwater inland estuaries and go along the shoreline at midtide (crabs stay around through the changing of tides and can be caught on both rising and falling tides; more on this point momentarily). You will see crabs carefully coming in near the edges of the shore to enjoy their scavenging, and, as a rule, they can see you as well. Thus when you see a crab you should swing your net decisively on top of it and turn the handle almost at once to entrap it; sometimes it helps to wriggle the net rapidly so the flustered, surprised crab immediately entangles itself in the net mesh.

I walk along the tidal creek looking either for the green blurry shape of a blue crab, or the flash of blue on his claw. Paddling along in a small boat through waters that have a fair amount of grass in them is also good, as the crabs are a little less apt to see you. By standing in a boat looking down you are able to spot crabs more easily than from the shore.

I also look for crabs—lately with less success, I'm afraid— around docks, particularly on the pilings. If there are certain docks in your area where men clean their fish (or scallops, if the water is warm enough through early fall for crabs still to be around) and there is a fair amount of waste being discarded, crabs will come to know the spot—for them it's the equivalent of a fast-food restaurant. Clinging to dock pilings is a favorite activity of the blue crab, so you have to knock it loose and scap it up at the same time. This method is actually a bit easier than scapping a swimming crab, which can move quickly out of the way. Using a longer-handled crab net, again lightweight for easier handling, helps when you do not have a handline but are depending on

Scapping

your ability to cover, say, 5–8 feet with a rush of your net more quickly than the crab can swim out of reach. The blue crab's rapid sideways movement in the water is paralleled on land by its relative, the fiddler crab, which also darts sideways with great speed, especially if it sees you approaching. One of the shoreline explorer's favorite pastimes is to watch the industry of fiddler crabs as they dig out their homes by removing miniature cannonballs of sand.

Remember that the last pair of legs of the blue crab are modified into paddles for swimming, and those paddles are very efficient. I tend to think that one reason the blue crab will swim close to the surface or near the shore so frequently is that it is confident of its ability to swim rapidly away from a predator—it just hasn't been equipped evolutionarily to cope with a long-handled crab net.

The blue crab is an aggressive and not easily intimidated opponent. When you catch one by scapping, you might even want to have a pair of tongs handy for grabbing it and disengaging it from the net because it will continue to fight with you to the very end.

Whether you are scapping by walking along the shore edges (the blue crab does enjoy resting in the mud in shallow water) or by poling or rowing along in a boat (with one person maneuver-

Fiddler Crab

ing the boat and the other person scapping), you will find after a while—once you learn to be very quiet, to put the net behind the crab if you can, and to move decisively after it when you do make your move—that it is great fun. It is also nice not to bother wrapping your handline around fish heads and chicken necks, so if you can catch as many crabs in either way, you might as well go scapping.

Trapping

Like most animals that man pursues, crabs can be trapped. Just as we can use a scallop fike to drag the bottom and entrap scallops, so we can set traps for crabs. We don't drag for crabs, of course, but we try to use our mechanical ingenuity to get them off the bottom with one kind of device or another.

There are different kinds of crab traps. The most popular are probably the two collapsible types made of wire and known as the star and the box traps; in both there is a flat bottom to which you attach the bait (again, oily fish or chicken parts work well), and then sides that collapse or fall away to become flat on the bottom. The point here is to have an all-flat bottom surface with a piece of bait sitting in the middle. When you pull the trap up, the sides come up and the crab is trapped in the middle where the bait is. The star trap, or pyramid trap as it is sometimes called, has triangular sides that fold up to form a pointed pyramid, while the box trap has square sides that come up to engage both the bottom and the flat top (which does not collapse) to form a cube.

A crab trap should be lowered into the water carefully so that it goes down bottom-first and does not end up lying on one of its sides, unopened. If there is a strong current, weights can be tied to the bottom. Usually the traps are set in murky or brackish water so you will not be able to see whether you have caught a crab, and thus you will have to pull them up every so often. On the other hand, you can trap quite a few crabs on the same piece of bait and bring up several at once. How frequently you pull the traps up to check should be a direct function of how well you are doing. If lots of crabs are around and being trapped quickly, you can bring them in and out pretty regularly; other times you may need to wait longer intervals. If you are not bringing up any crabs, move to a different location!

As with scapping and handlining, you need to pay attention to currents and tide conditions. If there is a strong current, and you are trying to capture crabs as the tide is going in or out with considerable strength, you need to take extra steps to be sure your trap is really open and flat on the bottom, and of course if you are not having luck and others are, you may want to move or make sure your trap is indeed on a flat-enough bottom, as opposed to a very rocky or shell-filled one, so that it is opening easily.

Trapping

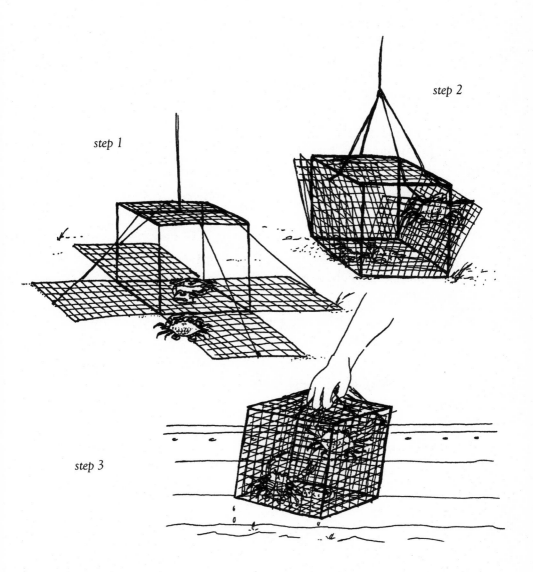

step 1

step 2

step 3

Most crab trapping is done at relatively shallow depths—say 10 feet or less. Many people enjoy lowering crab traps from bridges that cross openings of estuaries and creeks into larger bays. The simple crab traps described here are purchased easily at most marine hardware stores. If you are going to go after crabs at greater depth or with more serious effort, you will want to buy or build a crab pot, a more elaborate contraption usually with thin, screenlike wire mesh. An excellent description of the materials needed and the steps for building a crab pot are found in Lynette L. Walther's helpful book, *The Art of Catching and Cooking Crabs*. For the average recreational crab enthusiast, the traps are sufficient and are, really, yet another variation on handlining. You typically can control several traps at once, you are using bait and lines in similar ways, and, depending on your area, you will probably do about as well. I personally enjoy the direct feel of the crab tugging on the handline—a form of direct communication with the adversary. When you feel the line go slack, you go slack and let the bait fall, then hopefully feel the tugging start up again, and you respond in kind. It is a delicate interaction, and the fun of feeling steady pressure the whole time as you draw the crab to you is more satisfying than hauling up a trap to see what you have. In any event, it is good to be patient in either mode, even if at first things don't go so well. Consider the lines of Charlotte Brontë: "Life, believe, is not a dream/ So dark as sages say;/ Oft a little morning rain foretells a pleasant day."

Trotlining

For the moment let's assume that you become serious enough about crabbing that you want to go after them in large numbers, but not necessarily to set out pots for days on end. Trotlines are used to cover a larger area and to maximize your catch, working busily from a boat. This is not something I personally have done, but I can tell you how it works and encourage you to try if you want—it is going beyond the typical activities of recreational crabbing as I have described them thus far.

For many years commercial crabbers used trotlines, particularly in the nineteenth century. A trotline is a long line to which chunks of bait are tied at intervals of 3 or 4 feet. Instead of a handline with your hand at one end and the piece of bait at the other, a trotline has pieces of bait spread out in a line across the bottom for a great distance. For the beginner, a trotline of anywhere from 100 to 150 feet in length is fine. The same bait can be used, but of course even more care must be taken that the bait is well secured to the line, for the crabs will be hanging on to each piece for a considerably longer period of time. For this reason pieces of eel, chicken necks, and other longer "units" of bait that can be tied around the line will work particularly well.

To "run a trotline" you first create an anchoring device at each end of the line, usually with weights or chains, and have a buoy rising from each end of the line to mark the position of the line in the water. The trotline lies along the bottom, with the pieces of bait sitting at intervals, and then a line is tied from each end of line directly to the floating buoy, which in turn is secured to the anchor. It is much too cumbersome to tie the trotline to the anchor, for to work a trotline you are going along from a small boat, first letting the line out into the water carefully so that it can settle onto the bottom (it is a good idea to allow for as much as 20 feet of line attaching the buoys to the anchors, though you can use a trotline in shallower waters) and then circling back to your beginning point, indicated by the first float, and pulling the line in.

Creating your trotline can be fun, and certainly there is room for ingenuity. You can use cinder blocks, for example, as your

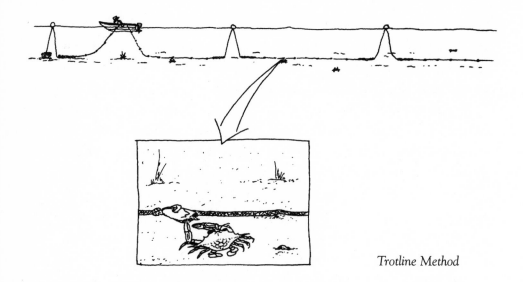

Trotline Method

weights. The line, usually about ⅜ inch thick, can be hemp or nylon. The bait can be varied. Many like using pieces of eel, as these can be tied around the line more easily. You can take a bunch of fish heads (by now you should have realized that you either have to have lots of fish heads around or know where to get them!) and, running a fishing line through the eye sockets, secure them very well to the trotline. Often people put the whole line coiled into a big bin of brine or "pickle" (4 pounds of salt stirred into 5 gallons of water), which will keep the bait fresh for several days, then go out the next day and "feed" the line into the water. Depths of 4–20 feet are workable. With steady work, you can catch a good many crabs, and indeed some commercial crabbers still use trotlines even though crab pots have become lighter and easier to manage (and are, essentially, foolproof). When you have dropped your first weight and felt it land on the bottom, you can let your boat drift as you let the entire line out, and then, of course, go around and begin to pull the line in.

As with handlining, when trotlining you are depending on the will of the crab to hang on to the bait. You must work with this will, as before, being very careful not to move too quickly. As you pull the line toward the boat you are again positioning your net in such a way as to scoop up the crab just before or, usually, right after it releases its grip on the bait. When you have finished getting any crabs from one "bait station," be careful to go gently and quietly as you begin to pull the line and advance the next piece of bait; as you go, you should be checking that each piece of bait is still well attached. Obviously you can replace any bait that is now missing. And as always, try to get the crab into the basket quickly. Chasing after a crab in the bottom of your boat is a pain, especially if the crab gets well under the stern seat or under a jacket.

Remember that both ends of the trotline must rest on the bottom. This is why having some chains at each end of the line works well, though if the current is strong, you may have to add some extra weight. By having a line of 20 feet or so leading to the beginning of your actual trotline, you can be sure to keep the trotline itself on the bottom, as that is where the crabs are. The anchors keep the line in a steady position and make it easier for you to work the line back and forth, and there is no need to move the line, for if the crabs are around, they will find the bait quickly. This activity is like handling a large number of handlines at once, though of course it must be done from a boat, whereas handlines can be operated from various spots. Although you can try using a trotline at any time of the tide, it makes sense to work the line in the direction of the tide, going hand over hand as you slowly pull the line in.

Using a trotline is not like many other sports I can think of. If you are bluefishing with an umbrella rig, for example, you have bait in a multiple display, but there are hooks concealed in every bait station. Some people set out trotlines with hooks when flounder are running. Trotlining challenges you to take the patience required in handlining and multiply it by twenty or thirty. On the other hand, you only have to pull in 4 or 5 feet of line— rather than, say, 15 or more—to see if you have a crab, and you are "fishing" with twenty-five or thirty lines simultaneously, which is hard to do in any other way.

Crab Potting

Although most recreational crabbers on vacation or out for some fun for a few hours will tend to either use handlines or go scapping, maybe drop some crab traps with collapsible sides, and possibly work up to the adventure of running a trotline, most will not get into the sport to the professional, commercial level of setting crab pots. However, if you wish to try your luck, I suggest that you first go out if you can with someone who is experienced. This will give you an idea of the rigor of professional crabbing so well celebrated in William Warner's wonderful book, *Beautiful Swimmers* (recall that the blue crab is *Callinectes sapidus*, with *Callinectes* translating from the Greek as "beautiful swimmer"). One of the many good points Warner makes, incidentally, is that the blue crab doesn't necessarily do everything on schedule! As one crabber remarked when asked why some of the aging females that go out to sea to die (as the rule is) sometimes return instead to their old haunts and limber along another year or two, "That old crab is hard to figure out."

If you buy or build a crab pot, you will have a fairly simple but ingenious device, just as with the lobster pot (see p. 105), and a very effective and reliable form of crab entrapment. The blue crab is quickly attracted to the bait and enters into the pot by crawling into the lower chamber, then, for its bad fortune, it moves upstairs, as it were, into the trap's "parlor," whence exiting is virtually impossible. Thus the crab pot can sit for a long time, having really captured the crab as opposed to having it hanging on to the bait, as with handlining and trotlining. The bait that is used in a crab pot is the same as the bait I have described previously. Crab pots can be set from a boat or dock and left untended or tended fairly regularly. Again, it is important to know and follow local crabbing regulations. In general, crabs should be brought up a few times a day. Commercial crabbers tend to pull their pots up every morning, remove the crabs, put new bait in the pots, and return them to the bottom.

Night Crabbing

A final, quite popular, and effective way to catch crabs is to go "firelighting" or "jacklighting." Sometimes this is called "night crabbing" or "night scapping." It is frequently done in conjunction with getting eels at night, and, like scapping, is another form of baitless crabbing. I have done this in a number of places, including Quogue and the Hamptons and South Carolina. You

Night Crabbing with a Flashlight

simply aim a flashlight or stronger battery lamp onto the water when it is dark outside. Crabs are attracted to light and will swim right into the circle of light your flashlight makes in the water. You then move the light toward you, the crab keeps swimming right along in it, and then you net it. It seems terribly unfair, in a way, to see how hypnotized the crab is by the opportunity to be in the limelight, though it also reminds us that humans are not the only ones with this tendency.

We are not certain why crabs like to go into the light. We know that crabs have excellent vision, that they tend to look directly into our eyes when we are trying to catch them, and it may be that they come into the light so that they can see better, determine if there is anything around to eat that otherwise might be concealed in the blackness of the water at night. You do not need any bait. The light is the bait. On Shelter Island at Louis' Beach there is a dock with lights on it, and in late summer the crabs come in and mill around in the glare of the light. You can shine a more direct beam of light on one when you spot it and move it around closer to you so you can have a go it at with your net. Catching crabs at night with a light is fun and is particularly a good setting for providing younger children with a different sort of "night out"; it's also a good atmosphere for telling scary stories. You must be very careful, however, if you go out in a boat at night. Also, be mindful of what the tide is doing. In any case, crabbing with a flashlight or lantern is a very successful method. You have an advantage over crabbing with bait because you are exercising a strong control over the crab's will, almost like hyp-notizing your adversary. When you see the olive or bluish green carapace of a large blue crab suddenly in your created circle of light, you feel as if you are being given a gift. That it will follow your light right to your net seems almost incredible, yet you could have this experience in Uruguay or on Cape Cod, on Long Island or off South Carolina. In many places around the world people will go out at night in small boats with a light and hunt successfully for crabs; here contemporary "electrified" man has a definite advantage over primitive man. Still, the numbers of crabs taken this way by recreational crabbers is pretty small compared to the commercial crab catch of anywhere from 20 to 80 million pounds of crabs each year!

Catching blue crabs is an inexpensive way to bring yourself into a wonderful and direct involvement with the sea. As is evident from my earlier book, *The Compleat Clammer*, I am a great lover of clamming—I dug my first cherrystones on the island one year on New Year's Day—and the feel of a clam in my hand cannot be overshadowed by any other saltwater experience; surely I am not in a hurry to handle a crab at all, but I must confess that catching blue crabs develops into a similar compulsive behavior, with each success whetting your appetite for another. Forget that crabs take longer to prepare than fish or clams and that, a cold beer notwithstanding, it can take forever (it sometimes seems) to pick the meat from a crab; forget that you may have one of your fingers raked or pinched by a feisty crab's claw when you try to disentangle it from your net; forget that you may kick this book off the dock and into the water in your excitement over netting a crab; forget that the crab is a mean-spirited, cantankerous creature associated (not without cause) with the wrong kind of grass and personality. When you have a heavy-pulling crab on the line, and it just doesn't seem to want to let go, however, you are happy.

3
Crab Cuisine

THERE ARE MORE WAYS to eat crab than there are to skin a cat, for no matter whom you meet and talk with about crab cuisine, inevitably you learn something new. In this chapter I will focus on some of the basic aspects of preparing crabs, introduce some conventional popular ways, and conclude with some further recipes you might wish to try. Since we are talking low in calories, high in protein, and delicious, you should feel free to experiment on your own and have some fun. But try not to overwhelm the essential flavor of the crab, for it is wonderful absolutely untouched. Crabmeat is pure and simple and is best when not overly integrated with other spices. One of the best crabmeat salad recipes I know is to add mayonnaise and a dash of pepper. Period!

Steaming (or Boiling) Crabs

Like lobsters, crabs must be cooked live, preferably by placing them kicking and snapping feistily directly into a steamer. You can immerse them in boiling water or steam them over an inch or so of water (some people like to make the boil from half water and half beer) on a steaming rack inside the pot. You can make your own rack by taking some crisscrossing pieces of pinewood that will fit in the bottom of your pot. It looks like a miniature trellis and should simply be rinsed off with warm water, not soapy water, when you are finished. You can even use a canning frame and put a rock under it, I suppose, though personally I don't see why it's necessary to keep the crabs out of the water. You really are processing them in a way similar to lobster, though whenever anyone arrives in the Maryland crab country and begins to boil a crab, everyone is aghast, for steaming them is the only way aficionados there proceed, always keeping the crabs off the bottom of the steamer and out of the water.

When steaming or boiling crabs (and I am talking about the hard-shell blue crab), first dump all the crabs in the sink and let a little cold water run over them, rinsing off extra mud or silt. Then, using long-handled kitchen tongs, transfer them to the steamer pot, with the bottom inch of liquid boiling away, placing them, again like lobsters, directly into the steamer headfirst. The boiling water will kill them at once. As you continue to fill the pot you will be creating layers of crabs. If as you pick up a crab to put it in the steamer you find it is very limp, there is a very good chance it is dead, so you should not eat it.

If a few claws break off, however, and the crabs are still alive, just keep all the claws and put them in the pot with the crabs.

Crabs themselves contain a great deal of water, so their own juices will keep adding to the amount of liquid you begin with; you can keep adding crabs to the pot and not worry about boiling them dry. Place the lid on the pot when you once have all of the crabs in it. It typically takes about a half hour fully to cook the crabs, and there is no harm if you run a little longer, since they are very wet in any case and that amount of time will cook their meat fully.

You can, if you like, add a few simple spices to the steaming solution. Usually you add a small amount of vinegar to the solution, as is customary when boiling lobsters, and a little bit of salt and red pepper can be added as well. It all depends on how much you want to do with the taste. Most people put the water and vinegar in, beer if wanted, then carefully lay the crabs in stacks or layers, using a pair of tongs (use long-handled ones, as this will make it easier to remove them from the steaming pot later) to carry them from sink to pot, add a few spices like "crab boil" or Old Bay Seasoning, cover the pot, and let it sit for a half hour as the bottom boils away. This is more than enough time to kill any bacteria. If you are boiling rather than steaming, 20 or 25 minutes is plenty of time. The boil can be pretty odorific and, depending on how others in the family feel, you may wish to add a few spices just to soften the strong aroma. More northerners boil and more southerners steam, but the crabs taste pretty much the same no matter which way you do it.

When you catch crabs you must keep them alive until you get them home, usually by keeping them under some saltwater-soaked towels, rags, or burlap when they are in the basket. They will stay alive that way a good long time. You can, if you want to, safely cook a crab even a few hours after it dies, but I recommend only cooking assuredly live ones. Why take a chance?

Crabmeat

Since Atlantic blue crabs provide some three-fourths of all the crabmeat you will encounter, much of which I am sure you will simply buy in cans of lump crabmeat, my comments apply to this variety. First, remember to cook the crabs live even if you are not planning to pick them open immediately. They will keep fine in the shell in the refrigerator after they are cooked. Indeed, nothing is more colorful than a display of red cooked crabs on tables of ice in open fish markets. (Lots of crabs are of course marked "live," which is ideal.) You can also pick the meat out and set that in the refrigerator.

The meat from the center of the crab (we will break one open in a minute) is the "lump" or "backfin" crabmeat; it is white and quite solid. There is also the white "flake meat," and the slightly brownish meat of the claws. Generally you will mix all of them together. You want only this crabmeat and should throw away the gills and intestines. To open the crab without pushing a lot of pieces of broken shell into the meat, it is simpler to use a wooden mallet than a nutcracker, though the latter used gently will work fine. The less shell you have to worry about, the better.

Most people pick crabs in the following way. Break off the big claws (1), and remove the meat (2). Pry open the apron on the bottom and peel it around so that you can remove the top (back) shell (3). Then push away the soft yellow material or "fat" you are looking at (4). Remove the other appendages (5). Break the crab in half. Set the legs aside to be picked open after you use your fingers to extract all of the meat, the bulk of which is the backfin and flake meat in the body. The bigger the crab, the more meat, which is why it makes sense, if you are buying crabs, to pay the higher price per pound usually asked for the larger ones—dollar for morsel, you come out a lot better, since the time it takes to pick a crab is about the same no matter what size it is, and if you can be pushing out bigger chunks of crabmeat from between the membranes with your fingers, you might as well be doing so.

Spread newspaper around on top of the kitchen table so that as you pick out the crabmeat you can toss the shells and non-edible parts (gills, apron, and so on) onto the paper and place the crabmeat in a bowl. Having an extra bowl of water around

Picking a Crab

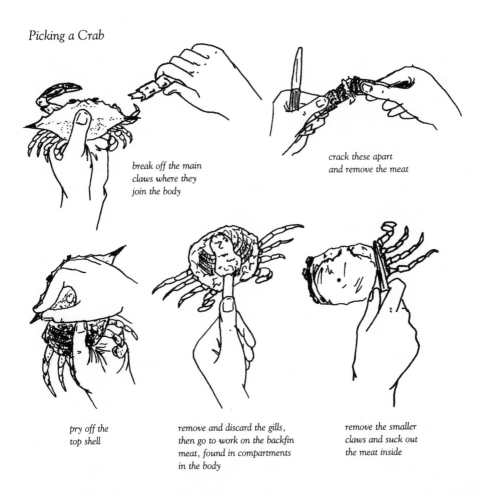

break off the main claws where they join the body

crack these apart and remove the meat

pry off the top shell

remove and discard the gills, then go to work on the backfin meat, found in compartments in the body

remove the smaller claws and suck out the meat inside

for rinsing your fingers every so often helps, as does having some beer or wine to keep your mood elevated if the picking begins to get tedious. Picking crabs is like picking raspberries in that you have to overcome your desire to put everything in your mouth the minute you pick it. Can you imagine a bear carefully placing each berry in a little container, or a fish setting aside some crab-meat? As animals we have to exercise great restraint and opt for at least a certain amount of delayed gratification, or else we could pick for several hours and have nothing to serve. Picking a crab does require patience, and as the proverb reminds us, "Patience is a virtue that few possess—some have a little, others have less." Of course if we decide we are going to "pick and eat," that is one thing; just decide which way you are going to do it and stick with it. If you are going to eat it, place a few small dishes (ramekins, ideally) of drawn butter around the table, along with some lemon wedges, so everyone can dip their pieces. If you want extra spices, have them handy as well, though I like to have the crabmeat, just as I do lobster meat, as unadulterated as possible. Crab flavor is incredibly sweet and delicate, so I don't see why we should load it up with hot spices—though I am not fully consistent in this regard, as I find myself opting for blackened, Cajun-style fish more and more often, most of which, my restaurant friends tell me, is prepared with approximately ten types of pepper!

Incidentally, most claws will require crackers or a small wood-en mallet to open, so be sure to have them handy. I generally open and pick claws as I go along, though some people prefer to set aside all of the claws and do them together, sometimes eating them as they go! You have, after all, four pieces of claw from every crab, and the trick of preparing the claws is to crack them rather than mangle them, again with an eye toward minimizing the amount of broken shell pieces that are loose. That is why a mallet has to be used only gently, not for smashing the claws. Your goal in cracking open claws and pushing the meat out with a knife, nutpick, or fingers (I've ruined a few stainless-steel forks by using one tong!) is to get the crabmeat out in as pure a form as possible, free of cartilage and shell.

If you are lucky enough to have caught or been given a few soft-shell crabs, those that have just recently molted and not yet formed their hard shell, you can cook them in a number of ways. It sounds a bit gross, but essentially you need to place the live crab on a board, make a cut behind the eyes, and then cut off the face. This can also be done with a pair of kitchen scissors. Next lift up the two points of the shell and cut or pull out the gills (you can then lay the shell back down). Finally, remove the small apron, wash the crab off, and let it drain on a paper towel. Then proceed either to broil or sauté it (see p. 77). After cooking, soft-shell crabs can be kept refrigerated several days or frozen for up to two months, though as with any seafood, I recommend not keeping anything frozen very long. It is better to stop crabbing when you have enough. The fun of catching crabs can be diminished if every time you look into the freezer you are reminded that you have bags and bags of cooked but unpicked crabs.

The beauty of soft-shell crabs is that since you will be eating virtually the entire crab, including its shell, you will not need to worry about picking the meat out. The first time I ate a soft-shell crab, after years of eating hard-shell crabs, I had trouble believing what I was doing. It seemed very unnatural, like eating a hamburger with horns or a fish that had not been scaled and gutted! However, the great taste more than removed my initial anxiety and I now am quite apt to order soft-shell crabs on a menu.

Just as I was a little worried about eating an entire crab, some people worry about eating the crab they pick. The yellow part is fine, it's the liver and should be blended right into your bowl of crabmeat. There is sometimes a little bit of meat inside the tip of the shell. Save that too. The backfin meat is the most tasty, the prized part of the crab, but don't stop when you have it out. Keep going. Work the meat out of all the compartments, and suck the extra meat out of the small claws. What you *don't* want is the thin walls (membranes) separating the sections, for this is the shell and cartilage material, the infrastructure that holds the body of the meat where it needs to be.

Even when you buy canned crabmeat you should go through it carefully and pull out any of these small brittle pieces, as they are very distracting when you encounter them when eating. By working with your fingers carefully, you will develop your own style of getting the meat out of the compartments as expertly as possible while removing as little as possible of the cartilage that you don't want. You can use a knife to divide the crab or break it open with your hands, in either case always trying not to send pieces of shell into the meat. Picking crabs requires patience, but the rewards are obvious. The price of canned crabmeat is pretty steep, but the work required is formidable and the taste unrivaled—except perhaps for lobster. In the nineteenth century and earlier lobster were sometimes known as "sea roaches" or "water rats" because they ate everything in sight and, in return, were picked up off the bottom and used as fertilizer. Consider the price per pound of that fertilizer today! And with crabs we also are concerned with a truly incredible gourmet item, well worth the price and well worth the effort.

A word of caution. Just as you do not want any pieces of shell or cartilage in your crabmeat, neither do you want any bacteria. Cooking the crabs kills all of the bacteria, but it is an often-noted important tenet of crab preparation that you *never* mingle cooked crabs with live or uncooked crabs. The point is simply that you do not want to risk having bacteria spread from live or uncooked crabs to the cooked ones that have been cleansed of any bacteria. Thus always keep the cooked crabs far away from the uncooked ones. This is why it makes sense to buy live crabs and cook them yourself rather than buying cooked crabs that may carelessly have been placed too near uncooked ones. If you are in control of the process, you can be sure that there will be no commingling. And for similar reasons, I think most people agree that it is better to purchase picked crabmeat in a can than in a container. It's best to catch your own crabs and cook them, next best to get live crabs and cook them, and next best to get canned crabmeat; finally comes buying, from a safe and reliable source, crabmeat that has been picked "fresh" by someone else.

In any case, assuming that you have either purchased some crabmeat or picked a bowlful, you are now ready to incorporate the meat into a variety of wonderful cuisine sensations. Let's begin with some of the more popular ones.

Basic Crab Dishes

Crabmeat Sandwiches

As with lobster, mixing crabmeat with mayonnaise, a touch of lemon, and a sprinkling of pepper results in an excellent base for a sandwich. Take about a 7½-ounce can or cup of fresh crab-meat, add a teaspoon of lemon juice if you like, and combine it with ½ cup of mayonnaise and pepper to taste. If you want to add bulk, it is fine to add ½ cup of chopped celery, cut fairly small. Some people like to mix in a bit of chopped apple as well.

A crab salad sandwich made from this mix is fine on either plain or toasted bread, and usually with a small amount of butter as well. If you like, you can make open-faced sandwiches this way and broil them. Adding a slice or some pieces of cheddar cheese brings another delicious flavor combination. You can use crabmeat-mayonnaise salad of this kind in a variety of ways, including making sandwich hors d'oeuvres. When we want to be a little bit fancy, we take a small fruit juice glass and use it to cut out round circles of fresh bread, white and whole wheat (the crusts can be saved for a bread pudding or put out for the critters!). Then we spread the crab salad on the bread circles as a great hors d'oeuvre. We also like to have crabmeat salad in hot dog rolls, again with a little butter and sometimes warmed in an oven. Next to eating crabmeat plain, I personally find a crab-mayo mix ideal.

Crab-Mayonnaise Salad

1 cup crabmeat	½ cup minced celery
½ cup mayonnaise	salt and pepper to taste

Combine ingredients and serve as a sandwich spread, hot or cold.

Crab Dips

Although some may not like the notion of putting crabmeat in a blender, or even of making a smoother, creamier hand-blended mixture from crabmeat, remember that flavor is the key point, and that there are some very quick and delicious crab dips to be made in this fashion. Essentially crab dips require you to do a little experimenting around several usual ingredients: sour cream or heavy cream; cream cheese; lemon juice; salt and pepper (although I leave salt out of everything and never miss it when preparing seafood).

1 cup crabmeat	1 teaspoon lemon juice
1 cup mayonnaise	salt and pepper as you like them
½ cup sour cream	

Combine all ingredients either by hand or in a blender and serve on toast quarters or with crackers. You can add more crabmeat to make it thicker, and many people add a spot of sherry, and sometimes parsley. You need to experiment a bit, which is part of the fun. You can also make crab dips by blending equal parts of crabmeat, cream cheese (1 cup of crabmeat, 1 8-ounce package of cream cheese), and a few other typical dip ingredients like sherry, lemon juice, Worcestershire sauce, parsley, and so on. It is pretty hard to go wrong, and after simply sitting down and picking a bunch of crabs, making dips and spreads out of mayonnaise, cream cheese, and several enriching flavors like sherry and lemon juice places you squarely at the center of some delicious simple crab cuisine. A good-sized crab will provide you with about ¼ cup of picked crabmeat, so figure four to five crabs to generate a cup, the usual base amount to make a sandwich spread or dip. And let's face it, you can simply pick open one crab, lay the meat in a roll, add butter to one side and mayonnaise to the other, squeeze a lemon over it, and sprinkle it with pepper to make one of the best treats imaginable. Certainly a sandwich or "crab roll" like that will go a long way toward keeping you motivated to continue picking when it begins to seem like something a little less than fun. And if you are watching calories and cholesterol, simply eat the crabmeat with a little lemon juice and a touch of vegetable oil to hold it together.

Crab and Cucumber Sandwiches

Crabmeat, like shrimp, goes very nicely with thinly sliced cucumber. I am always reminded when traveling in England that we tend to neglect cucumbers as a sandwich ingredient. In the summer of 1988 some other Yale alumni and I were served high tea by the late Kingman Brewster, a former president of Yale and then Master of University College at Oxford, and Mrs. Brewster. We arrived at 4 P.M. sharp and were served, among several other dishes, cucumber sandwiches. Bread, with crusts removed, had been lightly buttered, given a thin coat of cream cheese, and topped with a slice of fresh cucumber. To that you need only add a top layer of crabmeat. This is very good when served with shrimp as well, using one small canned shrimp on each little tea sandwich. It is fine to place a bit of parsley along-side as well.

You can also make a conventional sandwich by spreading one side with butter or margarine, laying down slices of cucumber (ideally you take the skin off, but it is not necessary), and then adding crabmeat with just a touch of mayonnaise. This is a very moist and delicious sandwich, taking the crunchiness of cucum-ber—which provides extra moisture and allows you to use less mayonnaise—and combining it with the flavor of crab.

Crab Quiche (Impossible Crab Pie)

Except that it calls for crabmeat instead of chopped clams, this recipe is the same as that for Clam Quiche that has proven popu-lar in my companion book, *The Compleat Clammer*. It derives from a family tradition of making quick and simple quiches of all kinds, and relies on another old family favorite, Bisquick. Many readers have enjoyed this approach and recently I was pleased to have it included anew in another East Hampton, Long Island, cookbook. Here's the crab version:

¼ stick butter

1 cup finely chopped onion

2 cups crabmeat

¼ teaspoon pepper

1 cup shredded cheddar
  (4 ounces)

1¼ cups milk

¾ cup Bisquick

3 eggs

Preheat oven to 400 degrees. Lightly grease 10-inch pie plate. Melt butter in iron frying pan. Cook onions, covered, in melted butter until soft and slightly browned. Add crabmeat and stir. Spread mixture in pie plate. Beat remaining ingredients until smooth (15 seconds in blender or, preferably, 1 minute with hand beater). Pour into pie plate. Bake until golden brown, about 30 minutes. Let stand 5 minutes. Garnish as desired.

Crab quiches, like clam quiches, can be made in this way and then frozen (assuming the crabs have not been previously frozen) until you want to serve them, at which point you simply warm them up. Readers of *The Compleat Clammer* recipe have also made the quiche ahead of time, frozen it, then found it easy to cut into small pieces to serve as hot hors d'oeuvres after reheating. In any case, it's an *impossibly* good dish!

Crab-Stuffed Tomatoes

You can serve stuffed tomatoes either as hors d'oeuvres, using hollowed-out cherry tomatoes, or as the main part of a luncheon, using either a hollowed-out larger tomato or, as I prefer, a tomato that has been sectioned open and laid back, with the crab filling placed in the middle with an ice cream scoop. To do the latter, you simply take a tomato and place it stem-side up, then quarter it downward and divide each quarter so you have eight sections, all just slightly connected at the base.

| 1 cup crabmeat | ½ to ¾ cup chopped celery or apples |
| ½ cup mayonnaise | dash of pepper |

Prepare hollowed-out cherry tomatoes or larger tomatoes, or use the opened-tomato technique. Mix the ingredients above as a crab salad, then place in the tomatoes. Garnish with a dab of mayonnaise and a sprig of parsley or chopped parsley. You can also add a touch of dill and a few slices of either ripe or stuffed olives if you like to make the whole package a little more attractive, especially if you are using larger tomatoes. If stuffing cherry tomatoes, no garnish is really needed except perhaps for just a touch of chopped parsley. Some people also like to add a tablespoon or two of chopped onions to the crab salad. It is generally ideal to serve a larger stuffed tomato on a bed of lettuce, and to prepare each plate ahead of time and let it be icy cold when you serve it.

If you want to serve stuffed tomatoes hot, cover the tops with a layer of bread crumbs (over the center) and, if you like, a bit of grated cheese, and heat in baking dish for about 20 minutes at 350 degrees. Again, my preference is to have them icy cold, partly because the tomato maintains its body instead of getting soggy. But to each his own palate.

Crab-Stuffed Avocados

You can prepare crab-stuffed avocados essentially the same way as crab-stuffed tomatoes, and you can have them hot or cold. In general it is best simply to halve an avocado, remove the pit, and fill each half with crabmeat, prepared as above. Alternately, you can peel an avocado and prepare a bed of slices over a piece of lettuce, then place a scoop of crab salad in the middle.

Sautéed Soft-Shell Crabs

Since I made these recently on Shelter Island for a summer luncheon and still have the wonderful flavor fresh in my mind, I want to tell you just how I proceeded.

I picked up some soft-shell crabs from a fish market in Sag Harbor the day before the luncheon. They had been brought in from the Chesapeake and cleaned live. I checked to see that all three necessary things had been done—the faces cut off (a flat edge where eyes should be will quickly tell you this has been done), the points lifted and the gills removed (by pulling up on the points and finding no resistance, you know this has been done), and the apron removed (quickly looking at the underside of the crab will let you see if it's gone; there should be a slight outline of where it used to be remaining as an imprint). The crabs were on ice and had just been cleaned, so I brought them home and kept them refrigerated until lunchtime the next day.

I held up the crabs and let a little extra water roll off them, but I did not dry them in towels or paper towels because I like to keep a fair amount of moisture in them (some chefs prefer to dry them more than this, so you will want to experiment). Then I rolled them on a plate of flour, being sure to get the flour in and around all of the claws. As I did this I was melting butter in a frying pan over a low-to-medium heat. I placed the crabs carefully in the large frying pan with the shell side down, used a fork to separate the claws so that the butter could get around all of them separately, sprinkled a bit of pepper over them, and also squeezed some fresh lemon juice. After cooking them on that side for about 7 or 8 minutes, I turned them over, and again added a touch of pepper and fresh lemon. I took the other half of the lemon and made two wedges to put on two plates, then about 7 or 8 minutes later served the crabs onto those plates and poured the remaining butter and lemon and flour mixture over the crabs, now a colorful red.

Eating sautéed soft-shell crabs is a great pleasure. For one thing, you don't have to pick the crab at all; you eat the whole thing except for the three previously removed parts. You have a variety of taste sensations—the crispy flavor of the small claws, the crunchiness of the main shell, and the delicious large lump of backfin meat that just sort of swells out beautifully as it cooks in the shell. You can serve soft-shell crabs sautéed in this fashion with various additions such as a tartar sauce, and you can cook them in a combination of butter and oil (they are a little rich the way I did them, using only butter) or, I suppose, just oil. You can mix a few bread crumbs in with the flour if you want. But taking the crabs and proceeding in a simple fashion as I did results in an extremely tasty meal. As a luncheon item, we simply ate the crabs, period, and then followed them with a large piece of cold cantaloupe (for a dinner we might have served a cold salad, coleslaw, sliced tomatoes, and a potato dish). Unless I catch or am given some, I can assure you I will be heading back to the fish market for more soft-shell crabs soon!

Broiled Soft-Shell Crabs

To broil soft-shell crabs you proceed in very much the same fashion as when you are sautéing them. First, preheat the broiler. You should let any extra liquid run off the crabs by holding them up and, if you want, drying them very lightly, then place them on a plate with some flour and cover them on both sides. In a separate bowl mix together softened butter or vegetable oil, or a combination of the two, a little pepper and a dash of salt, and a few tablespoons of lemon juice. Brush this mixture over the crabs and broil them on each side, about 2 inches from the broiler, for about 8 minutes, continuing to brush them occasionally on both sides until they are done.

Another way to broil soft-shell crabs is to make the mixture first, roll the crabs in it, *then* coat them with flour, and place them on a pan in the broiler. Turn them once, after about 10 minutes (again placing them about 2 inches from the broiler), and remove and serve. As with sautéing, it is best to wait an appropriate amount of time and then turn the crabs just the one time, rather than turning them over and over, the way you might a sausage. As when broiling lobster, you can always rely on extra butter and some lemon if the crabs seem to be getting a bit too dried out.

Crab and Cheese Fondue

Preparing and enjoying fondues is always fun and simply kind of "different." Lots of people don't realize that seafood and cheese combinations are great, although, as noted, people have discovered that a combined cheese and crab toasted sandwich is delicious. Having a fondue is, really, having a party, an indoor version of a barbecue, with everyone interested in getting into the action. It's a good idea to start with a soup or light first course, make a salad ahead of time, and then let everyone gather around a table with their wine or beer in hand. Some hosts like to serve a sangria or other punch, and generally the rule is to allow one fondue pot for every four or five guests. For a cheese fondue you can use an earthenware pot (since it's not that hot), a chafing dish, or your own purchased or rigged-up metal pot with an alcohol or Sterno burner set beneath it.

1 split clove of garlic	*pepper to taste*
2 cans frozen crab soup	*paprika*
1 cup milk	*French bread in bite-sized chunks*
1 pound grated Swiss cheese	*chunks of crabmeat*

After rubbing the garlic around the inside of the pot, place the soup in and, as you heat it, stir it until smooth. Slowly add the milk and continue stirring as you add the cheese. Sprinkle some pepper and paprika on top, set over the burner, and enjoy taking delicious bites. Most fondue forks can manage small bits of crabmeat, but of course you can substitute chunks of king crab or, if you like, lobster. By varying the kind of soup base, incidentally, and the main ingredient, you can have other seafood fondues, always alternating the bites of bread with the bites of meat. It's a great combination, and you can also add variety by using a different cheese.

Company Seafood Casserole

This is a very popular dish in several generations of our family and has evolved from a blender-booklet cookbook recipe by experimenting many, many times. More often than not, it is the dish my wife's parents, Robert Arny and the late Mary Arny, the well-known naturalist, used to serve to us when we arrived for a weekend at Shelter Island tired and hungry on a Friday night.

1 slice buttered bread,
  quartered
1¼ cups milk
1 8-ounce package cream cheese,
  cut in 8 pieces
¼ pound processed American
  cheese, cubed
½ cup chopped onions

1 teaspoon salt
½ teaspoon mace
½ cup parsley clusters
6 ounces wide noodles or shells,
  cooked and drained
3 cups crabmeat (or
  combination crab,
  shrimp, and lobster)

Preheat oven to 350 degrees. Place bread in blender and blend for 5 seconds on high speed. Set aside while in the blender you now combine the milk, cream cheese, American cheese, onions, salt, mace, and parsley (Mary used to leave the parsley out and just put it on each serving or the top of the casserole dish). Blend on high speed for 30 seconds. In a greased 2-quart casserole spread half of the noodles; cover with half of the seafood, then repeat. Sprinkle the buttered crumbs on top. Bake for 35–40 minutes.

Company Seafood Casserole is a very tasty dish, with the mace providing a nice balancing flavor that enhances the seafood (mace is a nice spice to sprinkle on bluefish, incidentally). Usually we have a combination of shrimp and crabmeat, and you can use either canned or fresh to satisfaction. This is a good casserole to prepare ahead of time and then have ready to set in the oven on schedule as needed. Mary found the shell pasta more decorative as a seafood dish, and you can experiment in your own ways, as our family has been doing for many years!

While we are on casseroles, let me introduce you to another of our favorites, this one first introduced to us many years ago by an old friend, Mary Cathcart, from Sunflower County, Mississippi. It was created by Lois Leigh and included in Mary's family church cookbook, *Bayou Cuisine,* and we have been enjoying it, as well as that entire very special bayou book, ever since we first had it.

Bayou Crabmeat Casserole

1 cup celery	1 cup mayonnaise
1 small green pepper	1 teaspoon Worcestershire sauce
1 onion	½ teaspoon salt and pepper
1 can crabmeat	1 cup bread crumbs
1 can shrimp	

Sauté celery, pepper, and onion in a little margarine until tender. Add other ingredients. Sprinkle bread crumbs on top. Bake 30 minutes at 350 degrees.

What could be simpler? It is a truly delicious combination, taking some of the same good flavor of crabmeat-mayonnaise salads, then augmenting with the onion and pepper in just such a way as to create a spicy and yet still very crab-dominated dish.

Hot Crab Soufflé

Here's another delicious hot crab dish we have enjoyed many times, after learning about it from our friend in Concord, Massachusetts, Kitsy Rothermel, who in turn learned about it from a friend in Maine.

8 slices bread	*1 cup celery, cut fine*
2 cans crabmeat (again, you can, as in previous two recipes, use half shrimp)	*4 eggs*
	1 cup milk
	1 can mushroom soup
½ cup mayonnaise	*sharp cheese*
1 small onion, chopped	*paprika*
slice of green pepper	

Grease baking dish. Cut 4 slices of bread into dish. Mix crabmeat, mayonnaise, onion, pepper, and celery. Spread mixture over bread. Spread remaining bread (cubes) on the top.

Beat eggs, add milk, and pour over casserole. Mix. Refrigerate overnight. Next day, to bake: Spoon the mushroom soup over the top. Add grated cheese and paprika. Bake at 325 degrees for 1 hour (serves 6).

Crabmeat Spread

There are many easy ways to make delicious crabmeat spreads, and they can be used both hot and cold. As with dips, you can experiment with a number of common ingredients such as cream cheese, sour cream, mayonnaise, onions, and dashes of

Worcestershire sauce and sherry. Here's one way suggested by Alice Canna of Connecticut.

1 8-ounce package cream cheese

1 6-ounce frozen package of crabmeat
  (or a 6-ounce can)

½ tablespoon horseradish (Alice
  uses more but says, "I
  can't tell you how much,"
  and we know horseradish
  is a very subjective affair!)

dashes of salt and pepper

1 tablespoon milk

2 tablespoons chopped onion
  (Alice uses an equivalent
  amount of dehydrated
  onion)

Combine all ingredients. Horseradish is iffy, so taste as you add. Bake at 325 degrees until heated through. Garnish with parsley flakes or toasted slivered almonds. Serve on plain crackers such as butter thins. We like to have this at a tailgate football party, as it is very spicy and hot on a chilly fall day.

Crab Fingers

Most people enjoy serving the chilled claws of blue crabs and refer to them as "crab fingers." If you plan on doing this, just make sure to remove the crabmeat from the claws intact very carefully, and keep them cold so they hold their firmness. Then simply set them out on a platter or in a bowl with a seafood sauce. We continue to make this dish as described in *The Compleat Clammer*, with a cocktail sauce.

Seafood Cocktail Sauce

2 teaspoons grated onion

1 finely chopped garlic clove

1 tablespoon finely chopped parsley
  (or parsley flakes)

1 tablespoon horseradish
  (or more to taste)

2 teaspoons lemon juice

½ teaspoon soy sauce (optional)

Combine and mix these ingredients together well, varying the amounts of garlic and horseradish through experimenting several times. Make the sauce a day or two ahead of time and keep it cold in a covered container.

If you are in a hurry, you can simply add horseradish to ketchup until it tastes hot enough. Crab fingers, like chilled clams on the half shell, are delicious with a little lemon juice as well (this saves you the calories). Either way, crab fingers are a traditional seafood party item, and while it takes a lot of crabs to have enough, for a special gathering this makes a wonderful addition to the table. If you want to make things simple, put a toothpick in each crab finger.

Maryland Lady Crab Cakes

There is an ongoing debate over crab cakes, with those who are purists being generally against the notion of doing to crabmeat what gets done to many other things with less éclat. Others find them a traditional way of enjoying crabs, and certainly they are popular in the mid-Atlantic states. I prefer clams on the half shell to deep-fried clams and I prefer crab salads and dips to the cakes, but they are nevertheless good eating and are typically found on the menus of many of the country's finest restaurants. The following recipe appears in a number of places in slightly different forms, and began, I believe, with an assist from the state of Maryland. As with the many other dishes described thus far, you are encouraged to experiment.

2 small eggs
1 cup seasoned Italian bread crumbs
½ teaspoon salt (I omit)
¼–½ teaspoon pepper
1 teaspoon Worcestershire sauce

1 teaspoon dry mustard
  (I like a little more)
¼ cup mayonnaise
4 cups crabmeat
oil, butter, or fat for frying

Mix the eggs with the bread crumbs, salt, pepper, Worcestershire, mustard, and mayonnaise, increasing the mayo if it still seems a little dry. Fold in the crabmeat and you should have a thick mixture to mold into crab cakes, which you place in the hot fat in a frying pan for about 5 minutes on each side. You want them crisp but not dried out, moist but not soggy. Making crab cakes is easy and fun, and you can make them ahead of time then just warm them up when it comes time to eat. I like things peppery and on the hot side, but you may want less pepper. You can also add a little more or less mustard and Worcestershire to vary the taste. In any case, Maryland lady crab cakes are a popular crab dish with many people and appear on lots of menus in the Chesapeake Bay area. And fortunately for both crabs and us, the overall health of the Chesapeake Bay improved dramatically in 1997, including large increases (5,770 acres) in underwater grasses, a cornerstone of the bay's ecological well-being.

Crab or Shrimp Casserole

For those who like water chestnuts, as I do, and the combination of water chestnuts and seafood, here's another dish from the Indianola, Mississippi, *Bayou Cuisine* collection, as worked up by Eleanor Roessler.

4 slices bread (toasted)	*1 can water chestnuts (sliced)*
2 cans cream of mushroom soup	*1 can mushrooms (stems*
2 or 3 eggs (beaten)	*and pieces or buttons)*
1 stick butter	*2 pounds crabmeat or frozen*
⅓ cup dry sherry	*crabmeat or cooked shrimp*

Pinch toast into small pieces and mix into soup, beaten eggs, butter, sherry, chestnuts, and mushrooms. Mix well. Add crabmeat or shrimp and mix lightly. Pour into casserole (or individual ramekins). Sprinkle top with paprika. Bake in preheated 400-degree oven uncovered 20–25 minutes, or until hot and bubbly. Serves 8–10. Fix a day or two ahead.

Fancy Crab and Cracker Hors d'Oeuvres

There are lots of ways to make crabmeat hors d'oeuvres to serve on crackers, and sometimes it is fun to dress things up a bit. Here are a few suggested ways. Mix crabmeat with a bit of lemon juice and spread on crackers you have covered lightly with mayonnaise, then garnish them with a little yolk from a hard-boiled egg. Another: Mix crabmeat with Russian dressing and a modest amount of chopped stuffed olives. Place a ring of hard-boiled egg white on a cracker and then place the crabmeat in the center. Place another slice of stuffed olive in the very center. Or again, simply spread a cracker with a cheese you like and then place crabmeat mixed with mayonnaise in the middle and top it with a small square of pimiento. Here's a salty one: Spread a cracker with sardine paste, then cover with a mixture of crabmeat, shrimp, and a little bit of sweet mustard pickle. A variation of that is to spread the relish around the outside of the cracker, then put the crabmeat mix, or crabmeat and mayonnaise mix, in the center, and top with piece of sliced stuffed olive or pimiento. The point is that there are lots of ways like this to make hors d'oeuvres that will taste good, look a little fancy, and spread the joy of crab cuisine.

Crab Bisques

As with lobster, a flavorful soup with crabs is always delicious. There are lots of easy recipes for making bisques, and here's one that has a quick and easy way of measuring.

1 can tomato soup   1 soup can milk

1 can pea soup   1 teaspoon curry powder

1 can crabmeat   4 tablespoons sherry

1 soup can cream

All you do is open the cans (crabmeat can be fresh, of course), mix together, and stir as you heat. It's best to put the sherry in just before you serve. Serves 6–8.

Here's another way to do it. Use a can of mushroom soup and a can of asparagus soup, 2 cups of milk, 1 cup of cream, and mix it all together with 1 cup of crabmeat. Essentially you can make quick crab bisques with any number of soups, tomato being the most common, but crab is so good that it goes with a lot of things. You can always add some cheese to thicken and give the soup more body. Incidentally, since "she-crab soups," of long renown, rely on using egg-loaded female crabs, which are illegal in most areas, I am not including them. Since it encourages people to break the law and keep "sponges," the egg-carrying females, the recipe seems pointless to include. Sorry about that.

Crabmeat Stew

It is easy to make a stew out of crabmeat (or oysters or clams or shrimp for that matter), simply by going through a few easy steps beyond making a soup. Shelter Island's late Captain Frank Beckwith would take oysters, crabs, or any kind of seafood and heat it in water in one pot, then slowly heat milk, with a little salt and pepper, in *another pot*, being careful not to let the milk boil. It won't hurt you if it curdles, but it's not as appetizing. When the milk was hot (you can add a few other spices if you want), he would mix the milk mixture with the water and seafood mixture, then add enough cornstarch to thicken it up. It's great with toast, or you can add some small potatoes and onions.

Crabmeat in a hot, thick, creamy sauce is delicious no matter what you do to it, and I am grateful to Captain Frank for having introduced me to the method of separately heating the water and milk.

Crab-Almond Spread

A very good and nearly lifelong friend of ours, Patty Dubin, makes this fantastic appetizer and, since it can be served hot or cold, serves it to us out on their boat when we visit them on Burt Lake in northern Michigan. It has become part of our annual summer reunion. When Patty's husband, Howard, cuts the engine and pours us all a glass of white wine, and we sit back on a summer evening to watch the sun set and catch up with the changes in our lives over the past year (generally an annual August ritual), nothing could add to the experience.

This spread should be served with crackers that are bland so as not to detract from the truly delicious flavor.

1 8-ounce package cream cheese	1½ cups crabmeat, picked
½ cup mayonnaise	fresh
1–2 teaspoons Worcestershire	1 teaspoon lemon juice
(to taste)	1 cup shredded almonds

Blend all of the above (using only ½ cup of shredded almonds) together, adding one ingredient at a time. Put in a shallow casserole and sprinkle with another ½ cup of shredded almonds. Bake at 350 degrees until bubbling and watch closely. If you like the bite of Worcestershire as Patty does, go on the heavier rather than the lighter side.

Crab Mold

Another great, delicious, and simple Patty Dubin recipe:

1 can cream of mushroom soup
1 8-ounce package cream cheese
1 envelope flavorless gelatin
   dissolved in 3 tablespoons
   cold water

1 cup chopped celery
2 chopped green onions
½ pound fresh or canned crabmeat
1 cup mayonnaise

Heat the soup and add the cream cheese. Add the gelatin mix. Stir until smooth over low heat. Add chopped celery, green onions, and crabmeat. Mix in the mayonnaise (make your own if you are so inclined). Put in an oiled mold—Patty Dubin likes to use a large fish (I'm not sure why, because it confuses me to have a crab flavor embedded in a fish form)—and refrigerate overnight. Unmold onto a plate of lettuce. Writes Patty, "It will be the talk of the party! Anyone watching their diet should stay away because once tasted, one tends to return often!" Patty likes exclamation points, as do many who enjoy crab cuisine. The following comes from our Shelter Island friend and one of the best seafood cooks we know, Libby Heineman.

Crab Newburg

1 cup fresh crabmeat
2 cups white sauce
3 tablespoons sherry
½ teaspoon salt

⅛ teaspoon pepper
1 teaspoon prepared mustard
1 teaspoon Worcestershire sauce

Mix all ingredients and heat gently. Serve on toast points. What could be simpler?

Crabmeat au Gratin

2 cups white sauce
1 cup fresh crabmeat
1 cup grated sharp cheddar
   cheese

salt and pepper to taste
1 teaspoon Worcestershire sauce

Mix white sauce and crabmeat. Add cheese. Season with salt, pepper, and Worcestershire sauce. Stuff buttered crab shells or individual baking dishes. Place in 425-degree oven and bake until golden brown, about 10–15 minutes. Libby points out that this is also delicious when you omit the cheese and instead add 2 tablespoons of sherry. Cover the top with buttered crumbs and bake at 425 degrees for 10–15 minutes. With or without gratin, this hot, steamy crab dish is the kind of simple but elegant creation that gives Libby Heineman such a far-ranging reputation.

Crab Melt-Aways

Libby is not the only one in her family who loves to create crab dishes. The following is a favorite of her daughter, Gladys Pinover.

1 package sharp cheddar cheese	*1 package frozen crabmeat (or freshly picked)*
1 stick butter	*6 English muffins*

To make this delicious party treat, simply cook the cheese, the butter, and the crabmeat together in a double boiler until blended. Then spread on 12 halves of English muffins (which fit perfectly on one cookie sheet), each cut in four pieces, cover, and freeze for 24 hours. Then when you are ready, simply bake at 325 degrees for 25–30 minutes or until bubbly.

Patty's Seafood Salad

One thing about Patty Dubin's seafood fare is her willingness to go for the gold, as it were, at least every so often. Sometimes she just decides to go big, make a fantastic dish, and then perhaps starve for the next week to make up for all of the indulgence implicit in one of her biggies. It would be hard to be served this dish and not think you are, as is said of joyfulness by some in California, "in the zone."

6 tablespoons oil

¾ cup chopped onion

3 chicken bouillon cubes (dissolved in 2 cups water)

¼ teaspoon hot pepper sauce

¼ teaspoon curry powder

½ green pepper, diced

¾ pound sliced mushrooms

4 strands saffron (or 1 pinch powdered saffron)

2 cups converted rice (use 1 cup of wild rice without seasoning packet)

5 pounds mixed cooked seafood (large shrimp, lobster, crab, scallops, whitefish, and flounder are great)

¼ cup red pepper (½ red pepper)

¾ cup Italian dressing

Heat the oil, add the chopped onion, and cook until soft. Add the chicken bouillon, pepper sauce, curry, and saffron. Make the rice by cooking it in this liquid mixture and bring it to a boil until all the liquid is absorbed. The rice can be a combination of white, brown, and/or wild, cooked according to directions, but at least one part of the rice should be cooked in the bouillon and onion sauce water. Add the 5 pounds of seafood, being sure to include crab, scallops, fish (Patty often simply microwaves some flounder), and shrimp, using large shrimp; all of the seafood should be cooked as usual ahead of time. Toss all together, along with the diced red and green peppers and the Italian salad dressing, and you are ready to have an extraordinary seafood salad where crab is indeed a partner rather than the main guest at the party. This is the kind of seafood extravaganza you can experiment with, as with making your own bouillabaisse or paella. Seafood tossed together with some good spices, in both salads and casseroles, leads to some adventure in the kitchen that most of your guests will be more than happy to share. Granted, this kind of dish can be expensive, but elegance is worth it once in a while—and, like Patty, you can always cruise for a few days once you have had the experience of being "in the zone" for an evening with a meal like this.

Whether you're working up crab canapés, making quick bisques, baking casseroles, or sautéing soft-shell crabs, it is clear that cooking crabs or preparing dishes with crabs is both easy and fun. There is lots of room for creativity, and it is hard to go wrong when working around certain key ingredients that so many crab recipes share. The combinations with such dairy products as cream, milk, cheese, and mayonnaise are time tested, as are the simpler lemon juice or seafood sauce approaches. Casseroles can be made in advance and heated up, and most of the cold dishes will keep several days under waxed paper in the refrigerator. Once a crab has been cooked and prepared, it is fine for a few days. Enjoy crab cuisine and know that you are in a very large company of seafood enthusiasts around the world.

Everything can lead to other things, as it were, when working with crabs. For example, crab spreads go well not only on crackers but also on endive leaves, snow peas, and cherry tomatoes. By taking a few cups of crabmeat and adding chopped onions, celery, a little wine and bread crumbs, and any spice you like, you can create a great mixture for serving flounder stuffed with crab, a popular menu item. You can carefully save crab shells and fill them with various mixtures of this type and serve the crabs themselves stuffed, just as you do clams. You can make some great combination seafood dishes using crabmeat and, say, mussels, or you can whip up a crab rarebit. There is no limit to what you can do with crabs, for they are simply one of the most versatile of all seafoods. If you are thinking of having a baked potato stuffed with crabmeat or an avocado and crabmeat mousse, do it! Just remember how much you like crabs and then you will have more understanding of why I have chosen not to include any recipes for she-crab soup. We need those crabs to keep coming!

4

On Lobsters and Lobstering

THE AMERICAN LOBSTER IS the robust king of seafood dining. As a seafood extravaganza it has been quite rightly lionized. Long prized and appreciated, always relatively expensive, the lobster has become an important part of our ongoing diet and has graced not a few tables for special occasions like birthdays and anniversaries. "Surf and turf" combinations notwithstanding, lobster really is the seafood equivalent of filet mignon. It has an unbeatable taste, a melt-in-your-mouth texture, and leaves your palate with the feeling of having been spoiled. We eat fish, and without reflecting any bias (I love most fish and go nuts over some very fishy ones, including fresh lake trout and whitefish from northern Michigan waters), we still often find ourselves saying that we are going to "treat ourselves" to a lobster.

The lobster has become a major icon for the entire Down East Maine coast, its likeness gracing, it seems, half of what is sold in Maine stores (just walk down the main street of Camden and look in any window), including dish towels, plates, mugs, and Christmas ornaments. The well-known Maine-life chronicler Louise Dickinson Rich has suggested that the gift shops in fact derive greater income from the lobster than the lobstermen do. She believes Maine lobster are popular because they live and breed in deep water, though she slyly observes, "The same is true of Nova Scotia lobsters, although this is not often mentioned in Maine" (*State O' Maine*, p. 181).

While the American lobster breeds and lives along much of the eastern coast of the United States, ranging from Cape Hatteras to southern Labrador, about one-third of all lobsters caught are from Maine, and about 60 percent are from Canada. Restaurants "fill in" necessarily with spiny lobsters, more abundant off the California coast and Florida, and imported from farther distances, particularly South Africa and Australia. But it is the American lobster that is celebrated and most widely sought out and appreciated (and that itself must look out not only for man but also for other such lobster-loving predators as skates, codfish, and dogfish!).

Ranging in size from about 7 to 35 inches in length, and from less than a pound to 45 pounds in weight, the American lobster is very prolific, but because it has such a complex metamorphosis, it is not as easily cultivated as fish (see Peter R. Limberg, *Farming the Waters*). Belonging to the crustacean empire, now some six hundred million years old (fish are only one-third as old), lobsters have survived through a series of adaptations and are able to eat an extraordinarily broad range of foods, including one another. Fiercely territorial, wary of other predators, they eat a great deal in order to grow, typically requiring about 15 pounds of carnivorous eating to grow a pound, as an incredibly high amount of energy is taken up in the very process of molting and growing new shells.

Lobsters like to stay cool and protected in the rocky shoals, hiding in nooks and crannies, digging holes and settling in to them, venturing out only to eat. They are very happy to sit under a rock for long periods of time. Molting is a key activity, with the female building up energy to molt every other year and the male every year. It takes the lobster anywhere from five to twenty minutes to molt, which it does by lying on its side and slowly breaking the membrane that joins its tail and body, then working its way out of the shell. It takes six to eight weeks for the new shell to form. As with crabs, the lobster mates shortly after the female molts, although as noted earlier, the process is somewhat different. The number of eggs produced relates to the size, with a 7-inch female, for example, laying about three thousand eggs and an 18-inch female, seventy-five thousand!

The American lobster is a wonderful color, a blue-green sparkled with blue-black and some orange on the pincers. All of these wonderful colors are from the pigment of the blood, incidentally, as the actual shell itself is colorless, made of chitin. With its two eye on stalks and its two pairs of antennae, followed by the wonderful appearance of its very large "club claw" and smaller "pincer" or "quick" claw, the lobster looks formidable even in the tank at the fish market. Hunting at night, snatching at fish and starfish, using its antennae to detect clams (it can dig one out of the sand with its large claw and crush it open, then dig out the meat with its small one), it eats much of the time. It has been called a "cheap-livin' fish," because it can survive on barnacles and mud, and even live in the bottom of a boat for a long time. Ogden Nash had this to say about the lobster's eating habits:

> I found the pith of allergy
> In Bromides tried and true;
> For instance, you like lobster,
> But lobsters don't like you.

Although not generally considered a particularly quick creature, the lobster can move quite rapidly, preferably going backward. When molting, it likes to hide in the grasses or in a crevice, but its powerful claws and snapping tail give it a lot of ability to maneuver, and its large claw can take off a man's finger, so don't be overly confident when handling one. They don't put pegs and rubber bands on those claws for nothing.

Unlike crabs, which as we have seen reach maturity in about a year, sexual maturity in thirteen months, and are therefore of good catching size relatively quickly, lobsters take a longer time to reach edible size. They go through many moltings to continue their growth. Laws need to be checked carefully (see the appendix), but in general the size limit for a lobster is $3\frac{7}{32}$ inches* from eye socket (say back of the eyes to be safe) to the end of the carapace. It takes anywhere from five to eight years for a lobster to reach about the 1-pound size that you generally want. "Berried" (egg-carrying) females may not be taken. My mother-in-law once saw a berried female in the window of a fish market in the tank and quietly went inside and told the owner, who had not realized, and who thanked her for alerting him. He could have lost his license.

The word *lobster* has had different explanations, including being tied to *lobscourse*, meaning "lap's course," a sailor's stew dish, but probably it comes from the Old English *lopustre*, a variation on *locusta* or locust. According to the *Oxford English Dictionary* the Latin word *locusta* describes both the lobster, or similar crustacean, and the locust. Certainly the French *langouste* for lobster (from an old Cornish word, *legast*) has long been the popular word for a lobster. The *OED* cites some other interesting early references, finding Sir Thomas Browne writing in 1646 that "lobsters will swim swiftly backwards," and the eighteenth-century

---

*It has been edging up fractionally in recent years.

English poet Gay noting, "On unadulterated wine we here regale, And strip the lobster of his scarlet mail."

The word *mail* deserves a special comment. I know I was once particularly struck, in visiting the armor rooms of Windsor Castle and Warwick Castle in England, by the similarity between armor and the shells of lobsters. Their appearance of overlapping connected and segmented pieces, which give a knight on his horse some freedom of movement while also providing protection, certainly evoke images of the lobster as well. Plate armor, it turns out, is often described as "lobster tailed," and small iron plates are riveted together in such a way as to provide for bending of limbs. But this association aside, *lobster* was also a colloquial name for British soldiers in their red uniforms; many lobster allusions in literature, incidentally, are extensions of the idea of lobsters as soldiers, both in their bright shells of armor and when wearing the proverbial "red coats" as at the Battle of Concord. Sometimes a policeman in a *blue* uniform has been called an "*unboiled* lobster."

In 1779 some Americans escaped from British prison; it was recorded about a hundred years later in the Vermont Historical Proceedings that "seven prisoners broke Prison from the grand Lobster guard at Fortin." It has also been said of a clergyman deciding to go off and fight in the war that he is "boiling his lobster," meaning that he is putting on the red uniform and abandoning his darker one, just as the lobster's color changes when boiled. If you are curious, as I was, this is why a lobster changes color when boiled: The dark bluish green pigment of the lobster alive is actually a complex compound between a protein and a carotenoid; when dropped in boiling water, the linkage between the protein and the carotenoid is broken, and the surviving color, red, is the color of the true carotenoid. It is like separating colors on an artist's palette. The change in the color of the lobster has been noted in various literary texts, but one that is particularly striking comes from Samuel Butler's *Hudibras* (II.c,21,29):

The sun had long since in the lap
Of Thetis, taken out his nap,
And like a lobster boil'd, the morn
From black to red began to turn.

There is always a chance of overcooking a lobster, too, as Lewis Carroll noted wryly in *Alice in Wonderland:* "'Tis the voice of the lobster; I heard him declare,/ You have boiled me too brown, I must sugar my hair."

My favorite literary reference to lobsters is a happy pair of lines—brought to my attention enthusiastically by my late father—from Byron's *Don Juan*, Canto I,cxxxv: "I'm fond of fire, and crickets, and all that,/ A lobster salad, and champagne, and chat." This says it all, despite the preponderance of militia-related comments such as Sir Walter Scott's "Oliver on horseback . . . charging with his lobster-tailed squadron" (*Woodstock*, v). Sometimes *lobster* is used as "a contemptuous form of reproach" (G. Jobes, *Dictionary of Mythology, Folklore, and Symbols*). To "lobster-ize" is sometimes used colloquially to mean to move backward. In general, *lobster* as a word gets most frequent usage when applied to other aspects of lobstering—lobsterman, lobster boat, lobster pot, lobster fishing, and so forth. To which we now turn our attention.

Lobstering has been celebrated as being both independent and demanding. Hauling traps up from cold waters, either by hand or mechanically, is hard work, and on a cold day it can be very fatiguing, but at least you are there of your own free will. It is some of this spirit that comes through in a very interesting account of lobstering written by a group of high school students with their teacher in Kennebunk, Maine, in 1977. In this book, *The Salt Book*, edited by Pamela Wood, we are given a good introduction to getting bait, setting pots, hauling lobsters, and so forth, but we also are given a reminder of the reason that many individuals, particularly in Maine, choose lobstering as a way of life: "Nobody tells you what to do or when to do it. You're your own boss." When the boats go out at dawn and drop the baited pots, then return midafternoon to see the catch, it can easily add up to a twelve-hour day, but nevertheless a day of self-control and self-assignment. There is a rhythm in lobstering, a spirit, that brings people into harmony with the sea. Considered a hard and demanding profession, it is also a satisfying and noble one. Putting out anywhere from 150 to 1,200 traps (usually 2 traps to each buoy), alone or in a pair of boats, from a 15-foot dory to a 36-foot boat, is hard work. When hauled by hand the lobster traps were made of lightweight spruce; with mechanical power now doing most of the commercial hauling, the sturdier oak is now used. In the olden days a man might hand-haul seventy-five to one hundred traps, but now he's apt to put out three hundred and haul five hundred to six hundred. The arrival of the hydraulic hauling equipment has certainly made the job different, but whether it has made a lobsterman's life any easier is hard to gauge. It still takes that native lobster five to eight years to reach the size to be kept—such lobsters are known as "keepers," as opposed to small lobsters or "snappers"—and if it is too big, you sometimes are not allowed to keep it, with regulatory agencies wanting to keep plenty of big "breeders" out there, which is to everyone's advantage, of course. Bait, whether red fish (ocean perch) or herring or something else, is still expensive, as are other costs. You have to enjoy lobstering to stay with it.

Just to get set up as a lobsterman you need to invest in a boat, traps, buoys, rope, a fathometer when you are still learning the depths of the area's waters, and various other items. Fortunately the license is not very expensive. Usually you need a bait boy or girl to work with you; often they will put the pegs in the claws of the "keepers" tossed in a tank, a large drum of salt water (which ideally is circulating by means of a pump). In the spring you look on the hard bottoms, in the summer on the sand (since lobsters go under rocks to shed, you need to drop traps near them to catch them when they emerge), learn how to fish near the shore in summer, move to deeper water later on when it's colder. All in all, once you have the equipment and some beginning knowledge, best gained locally through conversation and not through books, you can, if you want, go into the lobstering business.

My friend Jim Wilson of Westerly, Rhode Island, took up recreational lobstering many years ago. A rugged, strong seafood lover and gatherer, Jim sets his pots out in April and checks them every three days right through October; in July and August he tends to check his pots every other day. Jim uses cunners, a fish he takes out of the Pawcatuck River with a large dip net, or buys the remains of bluefish and flounder fillets. With the ten pots he and his wife are entitled to set, Jim takes in enough lobsters to serve them regularly to family and friends—and, as he says pointing to his firm stomach, "plenty of them end up right here."

Once, Jim located a small reef about 50 feet in diameter and marked the spot by putting a weight down with a float. He set a few pots down there and began hauling up regularly very large 3½- to 4-pound lobsters; unfortunately most of them were berried females and had to be returned. Still, it is worth keeping your eye out for a reef. You can, in Rhode Island, take eight lobsters a day by scuba diving for them, and a reef is a good place to look.

The last time I checked with him, Jim used double-header wire traps; they can be purchased in various coastal towns. Jim recommends the good traps made by Mr. Brown of Farm Home Road in Stonington, Connecticut.*

---

*The *Commercial Fishery News* regularly has advertisements for traps and trap-building supplies.

One final bit of advice from Jim: It is fine to freeze lobsters. The best way is to cook them and shuck the meat, then place the meat in a Zip-Loc bag filled with the water you cooked the lobsters in (let it cool first). Then place a second bag around the first one to ensure no leakage. Fred Kamfe, another good Westerly lobsterman who has shared his lobsters with us many a time, first gave Jim this idea and he's been enjoying frozen lobster ever since. As he says, with a touch of cheer and pride, when people come to visit him, no matter what time of year it is, "They expect lobster." Luckily Jim is good natured enough to give it to them!

Lobstermen are anxious to keep their trade a business and are not too interested in supporting the recreational lobstering that has become popular in recent years. Indeed, a certain amount of overfishing has made life difficult enough for lobstermen without any additional competition. Vacationers have been putting on scuba gear and diving for lobsters in rocky shoals off Long Island, parts of Rhode Island, and even in New York harbors, picking lobsters off the bottom. You need to check the area regulations very carefully before hand-picking lobsters, particularly if going at night with a battery light headgear. While lobstering is becoming more of a sport, it is still very tradition-bound, and recreational crabbers who would like to try lobstering would probably be best off to go to Maine and go out on a boat with someone several times to see how demanding it is. This makes more sense than going out and buying everything you need to get into lobstering in a big way. Crabbing, like clamming, lends itself readily to the vacationer or amateur seafood enthusiast. For lobsters, frankly, the local fish market makes sense.

The good news is, however, that you *can* go lobstering if you want to. You are free to set lobster pots and haul them, just being sure to check with the authorities regarding regulations, licensure, and so forth. And reading the book put together by the Kennebunk students is highly recommended.

If you are going lobstering you must familiarize yourself very carefully with the shoreline and bottom conditions, knowing where the rocky areas are, knowing the approximate depths, the unseen rocks that might wreck your boat, and so forth. Most marine stores sell government nautical charts that show depths, rocks, and other features of the water. If you can't find them in your area, write to the U.S. Department of Commerce, National Oceanic and Atmospheric Administration in Washington. Summer is the best time to try lobstering, as lobsters head for deeper water in the winter, but you can begin in April or May and work until October or early November if you want to. Before trying scuba diving for lobster you will want to complete a scuba course, typically including ten hours of lecture, ten hours of pool practice, several beach dives, and several ocean dives.

As with crabbing, lobstering is best done with fresh bait, and once again, fish heads are great, particularly from oily fish such as tautog (blackfish) or menhaden. (Fish markets will sell them to you cheap.) Let's turn now to lobster pots so that you can understand how they work. Other books are available that will teach you how to build a pot, but since I assume most of you are amateurs, you are probably going to borrow or rent or buy a few pots when you begin, so understanding them conceptually is more important than being able to build one.

The crabbing device mentioned earlier that my friend the late Ralph Grasso used for crabs amounted to a variation on a hoop net that originally served as a lobster trap. Essentially the bait was tied onto the middle of a net, the net placed on the bottom, and the net hauled up once the lobster had crawled onto it. Lobster traps have become a great deal more complicated over the years, although amateurs can purchase wire traps for twenty-five dollars that will last for years.

Lobster pots have "heads" or funnels that the lobster enters; it is enticed to do so because it is attracted by the bait, which is tied securely in another part of the trap called the "kitchen." The lobster moves through the head into the kitchen and enjoys eating the bait until it decides to leave, which takes it into yet another area of the trap known as the "parlor." Here its trouble begins, for it finds itself unable to get out of the parlor. Some lobster traps are "two-headers" and others are "four-headers." Some are round and some are square, with agreement that round traps are better if sea urchins are a nuisance. There are different ways to "weigh down" (sink effectively) a lobster pot, but three bricks usually work fine. Many traps are constructed now with cement portions built right into the "floor," which becomes a kind of home with its entrance, parlor, and so forth. The curious, somewhat artistic configuration of space has led traps to become popular as coffee tables. Restaurants find lobster pots decorative as well.

The best description of a lobster-trap head I've found comes from the Kennebunk book: A "funnel-shaped net tied inside the trap . . . guides the lobster to the bait. There are two different kinds of heads, the fishing heads and the parlor head. The two fishing heads are loaded on either side of the trap. The lobster first crawls through one of the fishing heads, goes to the bait, and then continues on to the parlor head. The parlor head is located in the second half of the trap. It is the last head the lobster must crawl through to be finally trapped." The net is now usually made of nylon, but in the old days used to be made of sisal (like jute). These old nets and other fishing nets would be dipped in tar; on Shelter Island we still have a "Tarkettle Road" where the large kettle of hot tar would be placed, and fishermen would come and dip their nets periodically. The wooden traps are heavy, weighing of course much more when wet than dry (almost twice as much, depending on the kind of wood), though with mechanical haul-

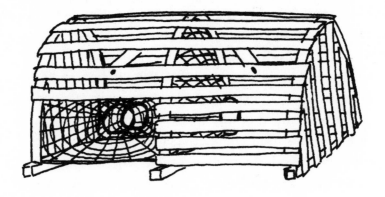

Lobster Trap

ing (professionals typically work as a team and haul five hundred pots every two or three days) they are not too difficult to handle. Wire traps are lighter.

Bait—usually fish heads or mackerel—can be secured to the inside of the trap in any number of ways, from tying with wire or cord, to hooks, to large rubber-band-like pieces of rubber, and so forth. The point to remember is that the bait will stay in the pot for a long time, so it needs to be securely in the right place within the trap to ensure that the lobster will travel through the head into the parlor. In his excellent guide to setting lobster pots, *Secrets of Potfishing*, Edward Ricciuti suggests that the line connecting the Styrofoam buoy to the lobster pot, heavy cord (typically nylon) of ¼ inch or more, be about 20 percent longer than is necessary to reach the bottom at high tide. In this way as the tide rises and falls and the currents kick in, there will be some built-in slack potential in the line so that it will not snap under pressure. On the other hand, you don't want the slack line to sit on top of the trap or get snarled on the bottom, so Ricciuti notes that you can tie a separate line, with a subsurface float, to the

slack line just to keep it from falling to the bottom. In this ingenious way you are really well covered for any eventuality.

When you have purchased your pot, marked it carefully as your
own in one way or another, rigged up a line, tied in the bait, and
spent a few minutes checking everything out to make sure the pot
is secure, the bait in the right place, and so forth, you are ready to
try your hand at potfishing for lobsters. With any luck—and again
be sure to check the local regulations—you will be able to secure a
steady supply of lobster throughout the summer months.

The easiest way, of course, to set a lobster pot is to drop it
over the side of a boat, and to place several in the same area, typically about 50 or 60 feet apart. When you head out to do some
lobstering, depending on how much time you plan to spend, you
might as well take some bait in one container as well as the
needed separate container that you will fill with seawater from
the side of the boat. And of course be sure to have a ruler or at
least a measure of 3$\frac{7}{32}$ inches or whatever is the legal size that
year to be sure the lobsters you keep are really "keepers." Be sure
you gauge them before keeping them!

The recreational crabber who decides to go after lobsters
should keep several things in mind. First and foremost, you
should remember that you are not a professional. You are out to
have some fun and catch a few lobsters. Since this means you will
probably be lowering and hauling the pots by hand, try to get
lightweight ones, not the larger, more heavy and durable ones.
Three to five traps will be enough for you to begin to see how
you feel about catching your own lobsters. If you want to be more
ambitious and set a large number, get together with several
friends and, as with a trotline for crabbing, let out a string of pots
over a straight line, then go back and check them sequentially,
being sure if there is no lobster in the pot when you haul it up
that the bait is still there (and if not, rebait it). If you are entitled

to five traps as a noncommercial lobsterman, with your spouse licensed you can set ten, or twenty with another couple. Be sure everyone pulls, as it were, his own weight!

In Maine there is a strict classification of lobsters by weight that is more or less the industry standard. Here are the names:

1 lb.—Chickens
1–1⅛ lb.—Heavy Chickens
1¼ lb.—Quarters
1½–1¾ lb.—Selects
2 lb.—Deuces or 2-Pounders
2–2¼ lb.—Heavy Selects
2¼–2½ lb.—Small Jumbos
Over 2½–approx. 4 lb.—Jumbos

Be *sure* not to take small lobsters or more than the legal quota. While the American lobster fortunately is not an endangered species, we must all be careful not to allow it to become one. Who would want, for example, to think of the American lobster in the same breath as such endangered creatures as the Virginia big-eared bat, the salt marsh harvest mouse, and the Utah prairie dog? And if you are not careful, you could be fined or go to jail, so don't succumb to the temptation to think that, well, once cooked, it will look about right on the plate. Use your ruler!

When setting your pots down, let them down slowly, going hand over hand. You don't want them to hit the bottom with too much force, risking either breakage or loosening the bait. When you pull them in, again go steadily hand over hand, keeping the line taut so the trap is rising bottom-down. Never touch another person's pot. Be sure your own pots are carefully marked, and if possible make a separate note on a piece of paper where you set them in case you have trouble finding them later. Some twenty years ago a few people in Maine were taking other men's pots.

After several instances of pot violations, the owners buried razor blades in the handlines at certain intervals that only they knew about. A stranger hauling one of their lines would slice his hands. Apparently that ended the problem, and while I am not recommending such activity, it stands as a warning not to break the law. Just as you cannot keep an undersized lobster, nor a "berried" lobster (egg-carrying female), so you must never disturb or haul up another man's pots.

Handling lobsters is easier than handling crabs. They are less apt to swipe at you and are easily grasped by the back, simply by placing your hand around the carapace. Never try to pick one up by the claws, and don't try to plug a claw until someone knowledgeable shows you how. Remember that a lobster can take off a finger; its claws are incredibly powerful. Professional fishermen peg or band the claws before putting the lobsters in a holding tank.

Once you know the regulations of the area you want to try lobstering in, you will quickly learn the hours you can go lobstering and learn to keep an eye on the tide. Depending on the direction of the current, you want to place your pots and buoys from the boat in a certain way, particularly with an eye to keeping your line unfouled as you let the pot down and to avoiding hitting the line with the motor. Also, be sure you familiarize yourself with the professional lobstering taking place in your area—amateurs are not readily welcomed, but they are tolerated more hospitably if you are polite, and don't place your pots in already staked-out areas. (For an understanding of the culture of professional lobstermen, see James A. Acheson's *The Lobster Gangs of Maine*.)

Boiling a Lobster

Assuming you have had some luck catching several lobsters in your pot, or alternately have been given or purchased some lobsters, you need to know how to boil them. This is not a big deal and not going to take up a chapter. But since so many people like to have lobster boiled and served with drawn butter, let's make it clear how you do it at the outset. Then I would like to describe how to steam and how to broil a lobster. These three methods are the most popular ways to eat lobster and everyone should know the basics. I will take up further lobster cuisine in a separate chapter.

Here's the plan recommended by the Maine Department of Natural Resources:

Take the live lobsters (a lobster *must* be alive until it is cooked) and place them in a large kettle (steamer, canner) containing about 3 inches of briskly boiling water, salted (or even salt water if possible). Some people recommend putting in a few splashes of vinegar—my grandmother always did this. (Some suggest ¼ cup of vinegar to each 4 quarts of water.) Take each lobster by the back and plunge its head into the boiling water so that it is killed immediately. Wait a minute for the water to regain its full heat and then put the next lobster in and so forth. The point is that you want to keep the lobsters completely covered with water; you may, as you add further lobsters, even need to pour off a little water to accommodate them all.

Cover the lobsters in the pot and listen for the water to begin to boil again. Then allow them to boil for about 18–20 minutes, turn off the heat, and remove from the pot. It's about twice as long as cooking spaghetti, except that given the size of your pot it takes quite a while to get the water boiling in the first place. Many people have invited guests over, then after a while turned on the water to begin boiling it. A large pot can take quite a while, especially on an ordinary-sized gas oven burner. I recommend allowing a good half hour to boil the water the first time, or all together about an hour to put lobsters on the table. If you are boiling an oversized lobster, a 2½- to 4-pounder for example, you should cook it for a longer time, virtually twice as long. In his recent book *Lobster at Home,* Boston chef Jasper White suggests a scale of boiling times depending on weight: 8 minutes for a 1-pound lobster, 9–10 for 1¼, 11–12 for 1½, and so on. He also suggests adding a minute or two if the pot is crowded and subtracting a minute if there is plenty of extra water. Take each lobster from the pot with a pair of tongs, hold it by the tail or body and let the water pour out, then set it on a plate or platter to cool, about 10 minutes. They will still be hot 10 minutes later, but not so hot as to burn people's hands when opening them. (Note that a freshly cooked lobster will have its tail curved under very tightly; never purchase a cooked lobster that does not look this way.) Before turning to steaming and broiling, let's review the main steps involved in eating a lobster.

Eating a Lobster

There are several ways to open a lobster to eat it, but I will go with the one I believe easiest.

Remove the claws by holding the body in one hand and twisting each claw full around with your other hand until it snaps off. Set the claws aside, and when you want to eat them, crack them open with a nutcracker. Usually one crack is enough. Don't squeeze all the way through the claw, just break it and then use your hands to finish. If you have a jumbo lobster it is a good idea to take a meat cleaver and carefully strike each claw several times. This way you make it possible to open the claws while also letting the water run out.

remove the claws

crack open the claws with a nutcracker, then use your hand to finish the job

arch the lobster until it splits in half . . .

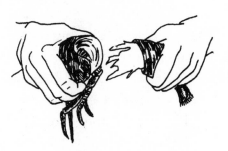

separating the body from the tail

push the meat through the tail

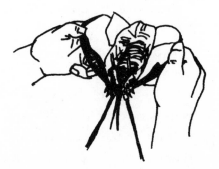

break or slice open the body and pull the two sides away from one another to expose many morsels of meat

Arch the lobster with its bottom toward you and apply pressure until it splits in half, separating the body from the tail. Most people then like to break open the body—a knife can be used to cut it down the middle—and pull the two sides away from one another. Eat the meat around the joints where the small claws are attached to the body, and suck out the meat of the small claws by sipping them like straws. Alternately, push the meat through from one end to the other with a small lobster pick (all in the same nutcracker set). When you pull the body from the back shell, you will find all sorts of little pieces of delicious meat, including the flaplike thin pink meat against the shell of the back, the "tomalley," or greenish-colored liver, which is a great delicacy, and the fluffy meat around the joints.

When you feel like bigger bites, start working on either the claws or the tail where the large concentrations of meat are. For the claws you can push the meat through or, by breaking open the shell from where you cracked it, just pull it from the side. The easiest way to get the meat out of the tail is to take a fork and push from the small end, working the tail out the large opening in the other end. You should be able to pop the whole tail out intact, then take bites of it interspersed with the smaller pieces that require more work. Incidentally, the flippers on the end of the tail that you break off before pushing the tail through from that end are themselves a good source of meat. Break each flipper open and you can pull out a delicious morsel, particularly in the wintertime when lobsters are fuller.

Basically, then, eating a lobster involves removing and eating the claws, pushing out and eating the tail, and working over the small claws and body for as long as you want. You can proceed in any order (as I hinted, many people like to alternate eating the easily accessible with the less accessible portions of meat). I find that if a lobster is still very hot when served it is a good idea to pour off any remaining water as you open each section, then go on to another, so that by the time your hands are actually on the lobster it is not going to burn you. In general it is a good idea to give a lobster a plate of its own, have a large bowl (stainless steel is perfect) for the "orts," the throwaway shells and scraps, and separate dishes for the other parts of the meal like a baked potato or a green salad. There is no need to cover everything else with hot lobster juice. Have a large supply of extra napkins and a number of dishes of drawn butter stationed around the table. It is a real pain to try to pass a dish of drawn butter when you are into your lobster. In fact you hardly want to stop and talk, much less pass everything. So make it easy for your guests by setting up the table in such a way that all anyone has to do is work on his lobster.

A few other tips on breaking open and eating a lobster. If you don't have a nutcracker set (or a pair of the increasingly popular and colorful seafood pliers), you can use a hammer or other strong kitchen utensil to break the claws open enough so that you can proceed by hand. If you like, you can cut a lobster's body straight down the middle *including the tail*. Many restaurants use a cleaver or large knife to split it in this way, but I think it is easier to keep the tail intact and then cut it up in bite-sized chunks.

Be adventurous about the body of the lobster. Most of it is good. You will find a few gills that are not, but don't be put off by rather unusual appearances. The bright red pieces are known as "coral" or unfertilized roe (eggs) and are very tasty. Too many people tend to eat the claws and the tail and overlook the great taste (and pleasure) of eating the rest of the lobster. Except for the shell, the gills, the craw in the lobster's head, and the thin dark vein that runs down the back (part of the digestive tract), everything else is edible. It is simply a matter of patience.

Personality comes out among lobster consumers, as some delayed-gratification types spend the entire evening working on the body and small claws while others rush to eat the best part and then concentrate on the wine!

It has always amazed me that a restaurant (compared to the fish market) can triple the price of a lobster by boiling it for you. It's not as if there is a complicated series of steps or a need to figure out exotic spices. We're talking boiling water. It is one of the easiest main courses in the world to prepare, and yet many people shy away from cooking lobsters at home. You need to own a canner, steamer, or large kettle (a pressure cooker will hold two lobsters of typical eating size) and have a stove and water. That's it. Some people are squeamish about plunging the live lobster into the boiling water, especially when its tail flips a few times afterward—this is simply a reflex action. Others feel their guests will have trouble dealing with an untouched lobster on the plate they are served, and if this is the case you can make it easier for them by separating the claws and cracking them, and by breaking the tail from the body or splitting it down the middle and displaying it lying on its back. I suspect that many people who enjoy having a lobster "out" don't realize how simple it is to prepare one at home, and, for the same price, you can have them several times more often this way, without worrying about spilling on good clothes (my sister made us all attractive blue plaid lobster bibs and we don't feel the least bit childish wearing them!). Even if you overcook a lobster, it won't hurt it. It is very hard to do things wrong.

When you set out to purchase lobsters to serve at home, keep several points in mind. You want them as fresh as possible. When you see them in the tank, and when they are removed, be sure they are moving their claws and, ideally, appearing stressed and feisty. Like crabs, lobsters must be live when you go to cook them. The dark mottled blue-green color of a live, fresh lobster is hard to miss. If someone holds up a lobster and its claws hang down totally limp, ask to see another. And know what size you want to purchase. Don't be talked into something else. For example, you usually want lobsters that are 1¼ pounds if you are serving one to each guest. Go for a 2½-pound lobster if you intend to split it down the middle and serve each guest a half lobster (which is fine and, in fact, makes cooking easier if you are having a large number of people). Once a lobster gets much bigger than that, the meat can be tough and the flavor not as sweet. Don't be talked into getting a huge lobster at a better price per pound if you want to serve whole small lobsters. If you are shopping for a number of items, make the lobsters your last selection. If you are worried about a fish market not having lobsters, call in advance and ask for some to be held for you. Then when you do pick up the lobsters, and you are satisfied that they are lively enough, dash home and put them in the refrigerator. They can survive there, out of water, for a number of hours, certainly for the afternoon while you are at the beach! If you go to cook a lobster and its tail, when pushed straight, does not snap back into a partial curl, consider it lost and get a replacement.

Although I will take up further lobster preparations in the next chapter, it seems best to mention here the other two principal ways of serving lobster in addition to boiling, namely steaming and broiling.

Steaming Lobster

To steam a lobster you should, ideally, use a large steamer, with water in the bottom and the lobster sitting "upstairs" in the waterless chamber. Of course in this fashion the poor lobster has first been caught in a multichambered pot and is now being cooked in another. (I will always prefer plunging a tail-snapping, claw-wiggling live lobster headfirst into a pot of boiling water.

But it is very easy to steam one.) Bring about 3–4 inches of water to a boil in the bottom, place the lobster live in the top of the steamer, and steam it for the same amount of time as if you were bringing one back from a boiling water pot, or about 20 minutes for a 1- to 1½-pound lobster, twice as long for jumbos. If you do not have a steamer, you can still steam a lobster in a very large pot by putting a small amount of water in the bottom and proceeding as before.

Broiling Lobster

To broil a lobster you proceed differently in that you need to split the lobster in half while it is alive. This takes a little more work but is still not terribly hard. Once you have made the initial cut, the lobster will die. The best way to proceed is to cross the claws above the head and make one fast cut straight down the body, starting between the claws. If you don't have a very good eye and coordination you can do it with a cleaver, but I don't recommend it unless you are willing to part with a claw of your own. As when eating a boiled or steamed lobster, you should remove the single dark intestinal vein and the craw (sometimes called the lady) behind the head. By holding the lobster firmly on its back and using the push of your knife as pressure to flatten as well as cut you can cut the lobster in half fairly swiftly. It is a good idea, regardless, to use a towel or a mitten in the hand holding the lobster down.

Once you have divided the lobster in half and removed the two undesirable parts, preheat the broiler and, while it gets hot, prepare the stuffing. There are various types of stuffing and you should feel free to experiment, but remember that you do not want to subtract from the wonderful flavor of the lobster. For example, take some bread crumbs (the main ingredient of all stuffings), and add the removed tomalley and coral to them along with a little melted butter. This method is recommended by *The Joy of Cooking*, along with a dash of sherry or lemon juice.

If you are stuffing the lobster (the state of Maine Department of Marine Resources suggests, for 4 servings, 1½ cups of cracker crumbs, 2 tablespoons of Worcestershire sauce, and 1 cup of melted butter—how can you lose?), you will only be broiling it shell-side down, typically for about 16 minutes. If you are broiling it plain, as it were, broil with the *shell* side toward the heat (same if using a charcoal or gas grill) first, for about 7 or 8 minutes, then turn it and place the meat toward the heat for about the same amount of time, being careful not to burn it. Broiled lobster is very good, and the intense heat seals in the flavor and of course gives a slightly crusty, chewy texture to some of your first bites. As before, you can eat the tail meat first, break open the claws when you want to, and suck the meat out of the small claws. In a way, a broiled lobster gives you more variety, as the claws will be very similar to boiled or steamed, but broiling the tail meat gives a special difference to lobster-eating experience. If you want even further variety, you can cut off some of the smallest claws and stick them into the dressing you have covered the exposed meat with. To avoid burning the meat, you can shield it with lettuce leaves, which you then discard before serving.

The larger the lobster, the more time you should allow. It is a little less scientific in terms of timing, but I recommend slightly overcooking rather than undercooking. Broiling is a way of having much of the lobster be a little crispy and drier in any case, so you might as well be sure that you have fully cooked it!

While a boiled lobster is my first choice, followed by steamed or broiled, there are some wonderful other ways to enjoy lobster. I have gathered some of the more popular ones together in the following short chapter.

Note that boiled, steamed, and broiled lobsters are all traditionally served with drawn butter.

Drawn Butter

Drawn butter is easy to prepare. Here's how: Melt butter in a saucepan completely, then let it stand for a few minutes while the solids settle downward. Skim the butterfat off the top and you have drawn butter ready to serve. (Individual ramekins are best and prevent various problems like butter dripping all over the table!)

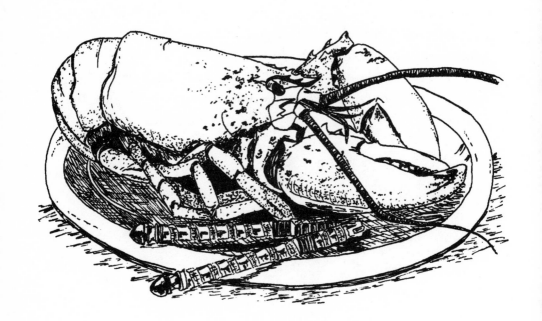

5

Other Lobster Dishes

WHILE MOST PEOPLE EAT their lobsters boiled, steamed, or broiled, there are many delicious lobster dishes for those who want to be more adventurous. The parameters of lobster cuisine are, in fact, steadily expanding as both gourmet chefs and individuals at home continue to experiment. Clearly the lobster is now well established as a versatile meal, and in this chapter I will both explore some traditional lobster dishes and point toward some new dining experiences. Lobster thermidor, lobster diavalo, lobster Newburg, lobster salad, lobster stews, bisques, and lobster as part of other seafood dishes such as a bouillabaisse or a jambalaya all have their place. And while some may feel that there is nothing more delicious than eating a lobster with drawn butter right out of its shell, there nevertheless are some very fantastic—and colorful—lobster dishes and combinations that deserve respect!

In all lobster cookery it is critically important, just as it is in crab cuisine, to work with very fresh and lively lobsters. Whether you catch or buy a lobster you want to be sure when you prepare to cook it that it is alive and kicking.

I am of the school that feels it is simple and delicious as well to prepare various lobster dishes *after* first boiling and cooling the lobster. However, there are many fine chefs who argue for working with live lobster, particularly if you are going to sauté big chunks of meat for a French dish like "homard à l'Américaine" or "bisque de homard." But again, it is fine to use cooked lobster meat (or canned or frozen). Cutting up a lobster by beginning while it is still alive is a bit more formidable than boiling or steaming a live crab (see p. 64), for you need to sever the spinal cord by running a knife into it where the tail and back are joined (and when preparing to broil a live lobster you first have to split it). That's just for openers. You can also hold its head under water for 5 minutes (in very hot, but not boiling water). Julia Child provides excellent instructions for this, in great detail and including illustrations, in her well-known *Mastering the Art of French Cooking* (Vol. II). Her account is the best I have encountered, and I might note that even she suggests you begin by holding a cloth over the lobster's head and claws, which heightens the sense of surgery I am not personally into. In any case, if you are working with a live lobster, be sure it too begins in a lively manner; don't start with a limp one to reduce the anxiety you may have about the task before you.

Now let's consider some of the classic lobster preparations you have either heard about or enjoyed and would like to try yourself. As with crab cuisine, you will find preparing lobster dishes relatively simple.

Classic Lobster Cuisine

Lobster Thermidor

There are lots of ways to make the dish, essentially chunks of lobster in a delicious, creamy sauce, with varying degrees of emphasis on other common ingredients like diced onions, mushrooms, peppers, and so forth—all combined and stuffed back into the lobster's bright shell, with last-minute runs under the broiler. Its appearance served in the shell is very bright and attractive. It is sometimes topped with a piece of bacon, browned slightly under the broiler right at the end (which is how we top off our stuffed clams—it's a delicious combination).

Thermidor is the French word for the months of the French Revolutionary calendar beginning July 19; it also stands for the overthrow of Robespierre in the French Revolution, in that month in 1794. The term can stand for that time of the year; writers have referred to "thermidorean weather" following in the wake of June. According to legend, the lobster dish got its name on January 24, 1894, in a Paris restaurant that prepared this dish in celebration of Victorien Sardou's play entitled *Thermidor*. The play closed after the single performance that night—but the recipe has had a very long run!

Here's a very simple way to experiment:

2 lobsters	*8 ounces chopped mushrooms*
2 tablespoons butter	*½ pint béchamel sauce*
dash of cayenne	*½ tablespoon chopped onion*
3 tablespoons dry white wine	*2 tablespoons grated Parmesan*
1 tablespoon tomato puree	*cheese*

Here is a simple béchamel sauce, as described in M. Soper, *Encyclopedia of European Cookery:*

| 2 ounces butter | ½ pint milk |
| 2 tablespoons flour | salt and pepper |

Melt the butter in a saucepan, stir in the flour, then boil the milk, add it slowly to the flour, and stir until thick. This easy cream sauce can be experimented with in all kinds of ways. A simple alternative is to take stock, butter, milk, and a little corn-starch and thicken it into sauce.

To prepare lobster thermidor, begin by boiling the lobsters and letting them cool so that they will be easy to handle as you remove the meat. Essentially you open the lobster just as if you were going to eat it, breaking the claws carefully and preserving the tail and the body (if you cut it down the middle) intact as much as possible; if you use the tail, it too is simply cut once down the middle (scissors are good for this). Remove the meat and set it aside, then cut it into chunks when you are finished, saving all the little pieces and using them too. Heat the butter in a saucepan, add the lobster chunks, the cayenne, and the wine (many prefer some sherry), and simmer and stir for about 5 min-utes. Add the tomato puree, the mushrooms, the onions, and simmer another 5 minutes. Combine with the béchamel sauce. Stuff the mixture into the lobster tail and heap up more on top of it. Sprinkle the cheese over the top, heat through in an oven, and then put under the broiler for several minutes.

While you can experiment with different sauces, including Mornay sauces, the point is to work the lobster into a nice mix-ture and stuff it back into the tail or into the tail and the central body shell. Thus you should be careful when removing the meat from the shell to try to keep intact and unbroken those pieces of shell you wish to stuff.

You can also simply sauté some mushrooms and green pepper in butter, along with the chunks of lobster meat and a bit of sherry or wine. Then add the cream sauce, salt and pepper to taste, and stuff the shells. You can add to the bulk of the serving by using some cracker or bread crumbs (plain), and you can sprinkle with paprika or garnish in other ways. The sight of a bright red shell exploding with chunks of lobster and other ingredients is a real joy on any table.

In fact you might argue that not only the taste but also the color of lobster accounts at least in part for its universal appeal. In Julee Rosso and Sheila Lukins's contemporary classic, *The Silver Palate Good Times Cookbook*, for example, they describe a very colorful "Lobster Fiesta Salad" that combines lobster with cantaloupe, plum tomatoes, papaya, and a few spices in such a way as to present a bright set of pinks, reds, and yellows for a perfect summer day. In similar ways, you should experiment with your own style not simply of preparing but also of serving lobster themidor, perhaps surrounding the bright red lobster shell with other colorful complements like lettuce, watercress, string beans, and so forth, In any case, for those who want to do something with a lobster and not lose sight of its body, as it were, removing the meat, doctoring it up, and putting it back in its shell for a delicious lobster thermidor makes very good sense!

Lobster Newburg

Probably the second most popular lobster dish is lobster Newburg, a classic dish, rich and delicious, that is made essentially the same way by most cooks. I will note a few minor variations, and once more you are encouraged to experiment, but in essence lobster Newburg involves preparing a sauce with egg yolks and heavy cream, combining it with a lobster and either sherry or brandy, and serving it over hot toast or pastry. Let's look at the essential recipe:

2 lobsters	salt and pepper to taste
3 tablespoons butter	3 egg yolks
½ cup sherry	1 cup heavy cream
¼ teaspoon nutmeg	6 slices buttered toast

Boil the lobsters, remove the meat, then cube or dice as you like. Melt the butter in a good-sized frying pan and gently sauté the lobster pieces for 4–5 minutes. Add the sherry and let simmer while stirring, about 3 minutes. Add the nutmeg, salt, and pepper (I prefer a lot of pepper).

Mix the egg yolks with the cream and stir into the lobster mixture. When fully blended, let simmer for 3–4 minutes. Pour the lobster over the buttered toast either on individual plates or in a large, deep baking dish. Serves 4–6 (you be the judge; you know how many lobsters you had and how big they were!).

You can approach this a bit differently by combining the ingredients for the sauce in a double boiler, and it is not necessary to sauté the lobster meat; you can just add it all together in different ways, the main point being to keep stirring and blending in order to achieve a nice creamy texture. You can put in a little less sherry and more heavy cream (some recipes call for 2 cups of cream, for example), and of course you can stretch the lobster simply by adding more liquid and, if desired, several tablespoons of flour to thicken it.

Lobster Newburg is delicious served over toast or poured into individual pastry shells. You can sprinkle a bit of paprika on the top. You can cover either large or individual servings with bread crumbs and give the servings a final few minutes under the broiler.

Lobster Newburg is a key into other kinds of Newburg, such as crab or shrimp or the very popular seafood Newburg that combines lobster, shrimp, and scallops, or lobster, crabmeat, and scallops. If using larger scallops rather than the small bay scallops, cut them in half to be more consistent with the typical sizes of the pieces of lobster meat. For variations on the texture you can use milk in combination with cream, and for flavor you can try mace or different kinds of sherry. You can also add mushrooms if you like. In any event, lobster Newburg served over toast or in pastry shells is a great taste sensation and, like lobster thermidor, extremely popular as a main restaurant entrée that is very easily made at home.

Lobster à l'Américaine

This classic lobster preparation is not for the faint hearted, because you are taking on a live lobster and almost wrestling it live into the frying pan. I'll look at the main recipe and then comment a bit further. There are many versions, but they are all essentially the same, and each restaurant chef, for example, has his own way of doing things.

2 lobsters (1½–1¾ pounds)
4 tablespoons oil
6 tablespoons butter
1 teaspoon thyme
4 tablespoons chopped onions
  or shallots

2 tablespoons tomato paste
dash of cayenne
⅓ cup dry white wine

You can begin by using a meat cleaver to cut the live lobster into eight pieces. Usually it works best to hold a towel over its head and press down firmly against a cutting board. The large pieces, all in the shell, are placed in a large skillet with the oil and butter already heated. The tail pieces will keep flipping around. Add the thyme and the shallots and, as some like, a bay leaf or two. Reduce the heat and cover for about 5 minutes. Mix the tomato paste, cayenne, and wine in a separate measuring cup and then pour it over the lobster chunks (remember, they are still in the shell). Mix together and let it continue to simmer, under the cover, for 10–15 minutes. Take the lobster pieces out and remove them from the shell, then return the liquid to the pan along with the yellow liver and the coral. Blend the liquids, add the lobster, heat, and serve (to 4 people, since you used good-sized lobsters).

Julia Child has no squeamishness and insists on using live lobsters when preparing lobster à l'Américaine. Her description of the dish is direct and colorful: "a live lobster chopped into serving pieces, sautéed in oil until the shells turn red, then flamed in cognac, and simmered with wine, aromatic vegetables, herbs, and tomato" (p. 224 in Vol. I, *Mastering the Art of French Cooking*). When serving lobster à l'Américaine you do not have to remove the lobster meat from the shell, but can in fact serve it in its colorful red shells and let the guests remove the meat themselves. You can, of course, use frozen lobster tails to make this recipe and come out in a similar place. In any approach, whether using live lobsters, boiled lobsters, or frozen lobster tails, you always sauté the lobster *in the shell* and you always rely on a tomato paste or combination of tomatoes and tomato paste. It looks very attractive when served in the middle of a ring of steamed rice. Lobster à l'Américaine is not for everyone when it comes to preparation, but on the receiving end, few will fail to be enticed by the combination of spices and the special flavor that comes from sautéing the lobster fresh in the shell.

Lobster Bisque

All kinds of bisques—crab, lobster, and shrimp—are quite similar, generally made with milk, sometimes bouillon or stock, and, unlike chowders, a minimum of spices and vegetables (celery and carrots, for example, are usually optional). Thus it is easy to experiment and not go too far off course. Most bisques have a few tablespoons of butter, a pinch of cayenne, and a touch of salt.

Bisque is a French word. It can mean a stroke (extra turn) for a weaker player in a croquet game; it is a term in tennis, and also in golf, but it usually means a creamy soup. Some make it with shellfish, others with rabbits or birds such as quail, capon, and pigeons. *Bisque* is also a glazed white porcelain, a *bisca* is a gaming place in Italian, and a *French bisque* usually means a crayfish soup! So you tell me. In any event it is a classic soup, and a classic part of lobster cookery.

1 cup lobster	1 dash of cayenne
¼ cup butter or margarine	1 teaspoon paprika
	3½ cups milk
¼ cup flour	¼ cup sherry, or to taste

Boil a lobster (or use 1 can lobster meat); pull the lobster apart into flakes and small pieces. Melt the butter in the top of a double boiler, quickly add and stir in the flour and seasonings. Stir in the milk and cook over medium heat, stopping just before boiling. Then add the lobster meat and the amount of sherry desired and keep it all warm in the top of the double boiler. In this way you prevent the soup itself from boiling and avoid having the milk curdle. You can change the creaminess of the soup in different ways. For example, you can use ½ cup cream, a cup of beef bouillon, and ½ cup dry white wine, then mix in sufficient chicken stock to make a less creamy version. Some people add a little boiled white rice to the soup; others put the lobster pieces in the bisque with the shells still attached.

Here's a way to make a lobster or crab bisque very quickly that will be delicious and take less time:

1 cup cooked lobster or crab	1 can mushroom soup
½ cup dry sherry	1¼ cups light cream
1 can tomato soup	½ teaspoon curry powder

Begin by marinating the lobster or crab in the sherry and then blending the soups, the cream, and the sherry. Again, heat but do not boil. Then add the crab or lobster (or both!). This is a simple shortcut and the results are excellent (based essentially on the "quick crab bisques" recipe in V. T. Hebeeb, et al., *American Home All-Purpose Cookbook*).

Lobster Diavalo

There are any number of lobster diavalo approaches; most are a way to have your lobster and your garlic and oregano too! It is a classic but somewhat less orthodox approach to lobster cuisine, certainly not in the same league as thermidor and Newburg, but very spicy and good nevertheless. The following is from *The Long Island Seafood Cookbook*.

1 lobster	⅓ cup peeled Italian tomatoes
3 tablespoons olive oil	oregano
1 tablespoon parsley, minced	1 clove garlic, crushed

Plunge the live lobster in salted, furiously boiling water for 15 minutes; drain. Pick out the meat and cook for 3–4 minutes in the olive oil. Add the parsley, tomatoes, oregano, and garlic. Let simmer for 6–8 minutes and serve piping hot.

It is interesting to consider dishes like this from a perspective that is more slanted toward traditional New England. It is a long way from baked beans, Indian puddings, boiled dinners, applesauce cakes, and corn muffins to take a lobster and work it up with tomato and spices like garlic and oregano. There is, however, a kind of naturalness in lobster cuisine that comes precisely from such crossovers that have nothing to do with New England, where, after all, lobsters are eaten so frequently that some even find them less than special. In her wonderful account of life on a peninsula up off the islands near Boothbay Harbor, for example, the well-known author of a good many books about Maine (see p. 158) Louise Rich wrote (in *The Peninsula*), "It will come as a surprise to nobody that the lobster, elsewhere a luxury and An Occasion, is commonly served in every household hereabouts. It's what you have when you can't think of anything else for supper, the local version of hamburger or frankfurters . . . lobsters are an old story, all in the day's work. Unless they are at the peak of perfection people here won't eat them at all." It is interesting to note that those who live in lobstermen areas and understand lobsters as part of their daily lives almost always eat them by simply boiling them in seawater, splitting them in half with a cleaver or knife, and dipping the chunks of meat in drawn butter. For all of the recipes that chefs have concocted, there is perhaps no finer taste in the world than lobster eaten in the most basic and traditional Maine fashion—for *most* of us, it really is what Rich calls "An Occasion." And in Maine they usually boil an extra lobster or two and keep the meat ready for the other dishes later, adding fish like halibut to stretch the supply for a Newburg, a sandwich, or a stew.

Lobster Salad Rolls

Most of us have enjoyed having lobster salad, either on round rolls, hot dog rolls, curled white bread, or open halves of English muffins. There really isn't anything to it—all you do is boil a lobster, cool, remove the meat, and blend it with mayonnaise, salt, and pepper to taste. It is a good idea to butter a hot dog roll lightly, then place the lobster salad in the roll, and sprinkle with just a bit of pepper and a touch of paprika.

Lobster Curry

As with lobster diavalo, you may find that the use of such a strong spice as curry takes you too far away from the basic taste of lobster; nevertheless, lobster curry dishes are gaining in popularity—along with most curry dishes (I just bought a bagful of curry in Istanbul's spice market, along with other favorite spices!)—and they represent an exciting new avenue in cuisine.

4 1-pound lobsters	dash of cayenne
5 tablespoons butter	3 cups boiled rice
2 tablespoons curry powder	½ cup cooked raisins or
2 teaspoons minced shallots	currants
½ cup white wine	3 tablespoons sliced, skinned,
4 peeled tomatoes	slightly scorched almonds
1 teaspoon minced parsley	1 tablespoon lemon juice
¼ teaspoon salt	
pepper	

Boil the lobsters for 5 minutes. Drain. Remove the meat and cut into small pieces, then place them in a frying pan with melted butter over medium heat and stir for 5 minutes. Add the curry, shallots, and wine. Cook for 5 minutes, then add the tomatoes, parsley, salt, and pepper. Cover and let cook another 15 minutes, stirring to blend fully. Serve from a hot chafing dish along with the rice dish, which is made by combining rice, raisins, almonds, and lemon juice.

This recipe is essentially the same as that offered by *The Long Island Seafood Cookbook*, and can be found in a variety of alternatives. Essentially you always proceed in the same way and you should experiment to taste, given the strength of curry. You always parboil the lobster, continue to cook it in the frying pan with the butter and shallots, then add the tomatoes (canned tomatoes are great to use if you have put them up in the late summer or early fall and you are now into winter!) and keep cooking as the curry works its way into the meat. We like curried dishes in our house and also enjoy bringing different kinds of chutney to the table, along with extra dishes of raisins and nuts, sometimes coconut shavings as well. Curry dishes are fun, and using lobster this way once in a while may get you enthused about experimenting with lobster dishes even if you like having your lobster in more traditional ways.

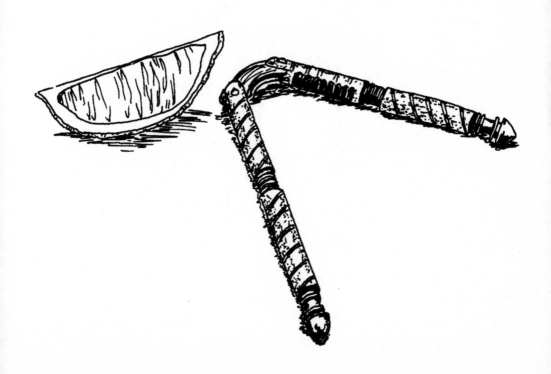

6
Crab and Lobster Trivia

❦

THERE ARE MANY INTERESTING peculiarities and perspectives on crabs and lobsters that are not the least bit important to our understanding of them, much less to improving our ability to catch and prepare them. Still, I believe we grow richer by way of such marginally important data, so it seems not without merit to include a final set of observations, fancies, anecdotes, and sundry phenomena in this little final chapter.

A Compendium of Crustacean Curiosities

Slow-Flying Crabs (and Fast-Galloping Ones)

It has been fun in the course of writing this book to uncover seemingly endless semantic and etymological variations on the word *crab*. Two that come together in a particularly curious way have to do with motion, and not the normal sideways motion of the crab that I have remarked upon (perhaps more fully than necessary!) in previous chapters. It appears that the crab was a type of airplane (an Auro 504K) used to train beginning fliers in the Royal Air Force around 1920. Because this particular plane was *slow* and also had a "well-splayed and much-braced undercarrier," it became known as the crab. Presumably it didn't, however, lay eggs. It also emerges that "crab" is a colloquial way of describing a horse valued for its *speed*. Consider this 1846 reference: "Out slides that eternal torment, Bill Sikes, in his new trotting sulky, with the brown horse he bought for a fast crab, and is mighty good for a rush," or again in 1846, "We had quite a few number of 'very fast crabs' here." A few years later, in *Vanity Fair*, appears this: "There is literally nothing that I can to do . . . except to smoke good cigars . . . drive my own fast crab, and keep a bachelor establishment." While crabs, then, were galloping fast and flying slow, other were still doing their usual bit on bay bottoms.

A Lobster, Not an Oyster or an Apple

One example of linguistic migration can be seen when we take a look at an old proverb, perhaps first used by Thomas More in 1557, "No more lyke an apple to an oyster." This recurs in various places, including Shakespeare's *Taming of the Shrew* (1594). However, by 1733 Fuller is writing "as like an apple to a lobster" (G. C. Apperson, *English Proverbs and Proverbial Phrases*). Surely this is enough to upset any linguistic lobster-cart!

Lobsters Yes, Spider Crabs No!

The dried carapaces of spider crabs (*Libinia* spp.), bleached in the sun, are probably as close to a science fiction movie enlargement of evil as we can imagine. And thus it is not surprising that spider

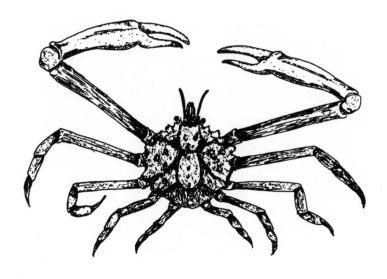

Spider Crab

crabs are a nuisance not only to recreational crabbers using hand-lines (some days I have thrown back ten spider crabs for every blue crab captured—and the spider crab hangs on, as if it knows you are not going to keep it) but to professional baymen as well. They are a particular nuisance when they show up in lobster traps.

Recently, however, scientific researchers experimented successfully at mitigating this problem. Fresh spider crabs were crushed and placed in the lobster traps right along with the fresh bait, and the result was that far fewer spider crabs were caught, as compared to the number caught in traps that had only the bait. The researchers, R. A. Richards and J. S. Cobb, concluded that the dead crushed spider crab parts set off an "alarm response" in the live spider crabs, thus confirming what we might have suspected, that none of us likes to lie down with dead of our own species.

News Flash: Vital Statistics and Facts

The lobster has a systolic blood pressure of 10, compared to 4 for the crab! Spector's *Handbook of Biological Data* also notes that the European lobster has a typical pulse rate of 60 (with a range of 50–100), about the same as an aerobically fit runner; the horseshoe crab slugs along with a pulse of 20.

The largest lobster on record, according to the *1998 Guinness Book of World Records*, is 44 pounds, 6 ounces, 3 feet 6 inches from end of tail fan to tip of largest claw; it was caught off Nova Scotia on February 11, 1977, and sold to Steve Karathanos, the owner of a Bayville, New York, restaurant. This record has not changed in the ten years that have passed since the first edition of this book, but that doesn't mean there's not a bigger lobster out there!

The largest crustacean is the *sanschouo* or giant spider crab (*Macrocheira kaempferi*), sometimes called the stilt crab, and it is found in deep water off the southeast coast of Japan. Although its body is typically 12–14 inches wide, its claw span is 8–9 feet! One was recorded as 12 feet 1½ inches and weighed 41 pounds; reports of others up to 19 feet have been made.

The smallest crustacean is the water flea of the *Alonella* genus, which is .0098 inch long and found in British waters.

Sand in Your Ear?

While a flea in the ear is often remarked upon, few of us realize that many crabs not only have a grain of sand in their ear, but in fact go out of their way to put it there!

We rely on the fluid in our ear's semicircular canal to maintain equilibrium, at least physically if not mentally. Many crabs, in order to have a similar sense of vertical orientation, place a grain of sand in their ear; when they molt they immediately put a new grain of sand in the new carapace. That this is their way of achieving a sense of balance has been validated by numerous experiments. Crabs are placed in an aquarium containing not sand particles but iron particles. After molting, they instinctively put a particle of the iron in their ear—and when a strong magnet is placed on the top side of the aquarium, the poor crab literally turns upside down. Best to keep sand out of your ear and stay away from giant magnets in any case (as explained in Jacques Piccard and Robert S. Dietz, *Seven Miles Down*).

What Traps Appeal to Peelers?

There is really no end to what researchers will do to try to improve things for their counterparts who trap for a living. In 1980 in South Carolina experiments were conducted to improve ways of catching peelers (premolt blue crabs), and variations in design and kind of trap were tried. Commercially caught peelers, incidentally, must be 75 millimeters across the carapace. "Peeler pots" with either 2.5- or 3.8-centimeter mesh wire and two or six male blue crabs were used as bait. "Habitat pots" were 30 or 45 centimeters high, and design changes were experimented with. The researchers then placed both the peeler pots and the habitat pots near one another at various spots along the bottom of the Wando River and checked every twenty-four hours, between April 1 and June 28. The habitat pots caught more peelers than the peeler pots. We can only conclude that for some strange reason there is less appeal for peelers in peeler pots.

Crab Pots Catch Turtles Too!

It is not at all unusual for diamondback terrapins to wander into crab pots, and although this happens with some regularity in certain waters, it has not yet had a particularly significant impact on the commercial terrapin catch. J. M. Bishop, of the Marine Research Institute of South Carolina in Charleston, has written up his research in "Incidental Capture of Diamondback Terrapin by Crab Pots" (1983; see *Oceanic Abstracts*, 1984). The fascinating experiments involved sampling of catches of terrapins in pots over four consecutive days over a number of summer months during 1979 and 1980 in several locations. Some 281 diamondback terrapins were discovered in the crab traps, and about 10 percent of them were dying. By daily checking of pots, drowning tended to be prevented. The "incidental capture" of diamondback terrapins in the pots of commercial crabbers were estimated at some three thousand *daily* during April and May of 1982. Clearly we need to think of ways to discourage the terrapins from entering the traps. Many a summer day when I am out clamming on Shelter Island a terrapin will raise its head near me and, after expressing surprise, sometimes even swim a bit closer. I savor such moments, as do others, so I hope we can keep the terrapins out of the traps.

When the Ferry Comes Through Lobster-Trap Waters

Maine has always been recognized as the center of the American lobster industry, and while we can speak of "progress" rather easily when more efficient transportation is created, it is fun to recall the reaction to having the *Bluenose Ferry* go back and forth between Bar Harbor, Maine, and Yarmouth, Nova Scotia, saving about 750 miles of driving for those heading to Canada. Because the ferry was *also* carrying, in addition to tourists and travelers, thousands of pounds of lobsters from Canada into the United States, the price for Maine lobsters was lowered. To add insult to injury, the large steamship also sometimes cut the lines between lobster traps and their buoys. One typical reaction: "My pa and my grandpa and *his* grandpa before him, all of us have *always* set our traps any place we damn well pleased in the whole Atlantic Ocean. And we'll keep right on so doin'! *Bluenose* or no *Bluenose*. If anybody's got to give way, let her do it. We were here *first!*" (Louise D. Rich, *State O' Maine*, p. 181).

Crabs Make Dutch Settlers Feel at Home in 1632 (When a Blue Crab Claw Waves the Flag!)

Lewes, Delaware, was founded in 1631 by a group of twenty-eight Dutch colonists sent to North America by a group of Dutch merchants, including ship captain David Pietersz DeVries. After a disagreement with Native Americans, this group was massacred, but DeVries was sufficiently interested in the area to set out himself in two ships the following year, arriving in December 1632 and staying until April 1633. He wrote a book to record his observations—some of it represents the best early natural history of the area on record—which was published some years later in Holland (1655).

Among other observations, DeVries was quite taken by the wonderful mix of colors on the large claws of the blue crab (we can safely assume the species from his description), particularly as he encountered them in shallow waters near "New Amsterdam" (New York). His reaction has to be one of the most personalized on record.

The claws of the crab—he had already commented on their taste and beauty—reminded him of the colors of "onse Prince-vlagge," our (his) prince's flag, that of the Prince of Orange, then the stadtholder of Holland. The flag, as described in an article about DeVries's book (*Estuarine Bulletin*, Winter 1958), had three horizontal bars—upper of orange, middle of white, and lower pale blue, all still colors in the flag of the city of New York. DeVries was probably made homesick, and he was certainly proud of his associating it with home, for he wrote that the similarity of colors and display could only mean that the Dutch "should colonize this country and that they have a proper right to it." So when a blue crab raises its front claw at you, realize that it is neither trying to fight off a predator nor grab for food but indeed simply waving the Dutch colors for you.

Start Another Claw, Please!

I'm not certain there is any real conviction in the old proverb, "The older the crab, the tougher the claw." It is not at all trivial, really, but blue crabs like the other crabs enjoy the benefits of autonomy—that is, the process by which when a limb is torn off, it can be replaced. A membrane quickly closes the wounded spot where the limb was attached, and this membrane becomes the capsule of the new limb bud, which holds the new appendage during regeneration. This process is in turn controlled by the nervous system working together with various environmental factors such as temperature and light. Of course when you combine regeneration with creatures that molt, you can have limbs torn off at various stages and sometimes be replacing things from several different perspectives, as it were; thus we find many claw deformities. There are often extra appendages or parts thereof on crabs and lobsters; in general, though, it is better to have more rather than less, and of course if a crab could wave three instead of two flags of the Prince of Orange, well, what could be more loyal?

Fiddler Crabs: The New "Supermales"

There is presently a scholarly debate taking place regarding "supermale" fiddler crabs, those that have been turning up with two large claws (usually the male has one large and one small, the female two small; the new breed has two large). Some believe that the new crabs may represent a new breed, though scientifically this has not been proven. More likely is the theory put forward by Monica Tzinas.* Basically, she takes off from research proving that sometimes a torn-off claw or limb regenerates into one of a different size. Sometimes the large and small claws can even exchange places! There are strange differences in the growth rates of normal limbs and replacement limbs. In any case, it is hard to imagine the fiddler crab eating carefully with two large claws, which is why Ms. Tzinas speculates that the supermales may be feeding in interstitial waters, which are loaded with bacteria that can be eaten without being picked up.

Playing Fiddler Crab

I guess all of us like to act out an occasional fantasy, and sometimes the borderlines between fantasy and scientific research can become a bit blurred. Take the case of Gilbert Klingel, a naturalist writing some twenty years ago, who decided that the only way to get a good perspective on the world of the fiddler crab was to become one. Here is his description:

"For the space of a half hour between seven and eight o'clock one summer evening I lay on the sand near the mouth of the Rappahannock River in Virginia and tried to imagine what it was like to be a Chesapeake Bay Fiddler Crab. This proved to be a highly unscientific, wholly undignified, yet entertaining proceed-

---

*"Supermale Fiddler Crab—A New Form?", *Underwater Naturalist*, Vol. 17, No. 3, pp. 24–25.

ing. In order to secure the proper perspective it was necessary to lie prone, half buried between land and water, and so adjusted that my eyes were but an inch or so above sea level. At this height the world took on new dimensions and assumed in the half-light of evening an aspect so unreal as to appear slightly Martian."

Although we might have more trouble acting out the perspective of a lobster (say by submerging ourselves in scuba gear and sitting under a rock on the ocean floor for an hour) or of a blue crab (perhaps asking several friends to tie a huge steak on a long string, which you could sink your teeth into 100 miles offshore and let them pull you slowly in on their handline), it cannot be denied that we may learn something from such attempts to become the quarry, to think as they think. And as Klingel notes, "It is a revealing commentary on the steadfast habits of the human race that not one person in ten thousand can even think of looking at his surroundings except from the long-established adult elevation of between five and six feet." Accordingly, I recommend that everyone try their claw at perhaps one such experiment.

Low-Cholesterol Diets for Lobsters

While we are interested in eating lobsters, and perhaps in knowing that they are low in cholesterol (the butter you have with them is another story), scientists are interested in the lobsters' cholesterol intake and are experimenting, with interesting results. Researchers at the University of California at Davis have compared purified diets and unrefined diets in *Homarus americanus*. Purified diets led to weight increases of 30 percent of the increases registered on a live food diet, with similar high survival rates. And one diet in particular, which leaned heavily on the use of an astaxanthin concentrate derived from crayfish waste, "enhanced growth significantly, and all the diets tested promoted growth and survival with only 0.2% dietary cholesterol" (*Oceanic Abstracts,*

Vol. 25, No. 2, April 1988). And they didn't even need to eliminate bacon. Of course, crayfish waste may not be your first choice. . . .

Exotic Lobster Dishes

For those who might wish to create truly exotic lobster dishes, beyond awesome to the zone of clawsome, I recommend working through *The Garland Recipe Index* (K. Torgeson and S. Weinstein, Garland Publishing, N.Y. and London, 1984). Here you will be given guidance to such fare as lobster in absinthe, lobster "arch-duke" (stuffed in a cream sauce), lobster in seaweed, lobster Cantonese, lobster soufflés, lobster stir-fried, and, of course, lobster with baby eels.

Behind the Crab Count

Ever wonder how we determine just how many crabs are caught? So do a lot of other people, and indeed there are many critics of the estimates of commercial fishery numbers. Fishing statistics are always going to be questionable. Presently researchers are estimating "sources of bias," for example in the commercial harvest estimation systems in Maryland and Virginia. The Maryland Department of Natural Resources mails out a monthly questionnaire, using a "stratified random sampling design" to gauge the numbers.

Crab Plover, Crab Spider, et al.

There are various other creatures in the world that have a relationship to crabs and thus incorporate the word *crab* in their own names. There is the crab plover, a handsome black-and-white bird about 16 inches long that frequents the coast of the Indian Ocean. Tame but noisy, it spends its time hunting for mollusks and crabs, which it breaks with its beak. We know about the spider crab, but what about the crab spider? From the family Thomasidae (order of Araneida), this spider is crablike in its shape and walks sideways or backward, same as the crab. The crab spider is found all over the world—there are 125 species in the United States alone—and catches its food not by spinning a web but simply by waiting in hiding for unsuspecting prey. There is also the crabeater seal of the Antarctic, which despite its name doesn't eat crabs but krill (planktonic crustaceans and larvae), and the crab-eating fox, a member of the dog family, also known as the crab-eating dog and the Savanna fox. This crabber is found in South America. Crabs clearly form part of the diet or inspiration for many other occupants of the earth, and man is no exception, just one of the bunch.

Crabs and Music: Melody Backward

Yes, crabs make it into music as well, albeit in their usual backward fashion (note the old adage, "He who goes with crabs learns to walk backward"). A "canon" in music is a piece in which one voice begins, then is imitated note for note by a different voice or part, which begins later and then overlaps the first (the double and triple canons of Benjamin Britten's "Ceremony of Carols" are my favorites). In one particular form, the second or imitating voice produces the melody *backward*; here the notes begin together and then go in opposite directions, leading to the name "crab-canon." In German this musical oddity is known as the *Krebs-Canon*. In more esoteric circles it is referred to as the "Canon Recte et Retro" or "Rectus et Invertus," to reflect its forward and backward pairing. And as you might guess, the poor crab gets it in the negative once again, as in this summary commentary from *The Oxford Companion to Music*: "This type of canon, however much it may contribute to the pride of its contriver, is necessarily artificially futile, since no listener can possibly discover what is going on, a melody sung backwards being in effect a new melody, and not being (by the ear) recognizably related to its original self." So sing a crab-canon at your risk, and when in the mood perhaps to be a little perverse. It might be appropriate to start your fun with the familiar canon of "Row, row, row your boat!"

What's in a Name?

This could keep you from asking an embarrassing question, especially if you are starting to talk with a professional lobster fisherman. Unlike the eel (elver), the deer (fawn), and let's pick the kangaroo (joey), a little lobster is called by the same name as a big lobster. A lobster is a lobster is a lobster.

Net Benefits: Regulating Lobster Regulations

It is well known that lobstering "used to be better." Overfishing, particularly in the early years of this century, has greatly reduced the supply of lobsters. "Time was," as they might express it in Maine, that you could trap more and bigger lobsters in far less time than you can today. Thus it becomes very important to review and study lobster regulations. Are we going about regulating lobstering activities in the best way? Considerable study of this issue is taking place, all with an eye to discovering whether by changing the regulations we can improve the catch, particularly for professional lobstermen.

Researchers at the University of Rhode Island designed a simulation model to test certain aspects of the American lobster fishery management plan. They found that it makes sense to increase the minimum size for keeping lobsters that are trapped while simultaneously reducing the aggregate fishing mortality. Together these steps are "economically justified in the sense that net bene-fits are positive: increasing the minimum size without an adjunct regulation to prohibit entry will cause present fishermen to suffer an initial short-term reduction in revenues for which there will be no long-term gain; and a program of effort reduction which reduces by 20% the fraction of available lobsters captured annu-ally is projected to generate $1 of producer benefits for every pound of lobster landed" (from *Oceanic Abstracts*, Vol. 25, No. 1, p. 122). In sum, we all come out better if we insist on catching slightly bigger lobsters in slightly smaller numbers.

Scientists elsewhere have been studying what they refer to as "nondestructive" methods of measuring the growth in lobsters— for instance, weight wet in the air, displacement volume in water—with regard to how they correlate with the "destructive" methods—where the lobster needs to be kept—such as dry weight and total body protein level. Obviously we'd like to see them concentrate on the nondestructive methods.

One thing is certain: We all want to be able to eat as much lobster as possible in the future. The review of regulations is wel-come. So are experiments—which would surely surprise the set-tlers who once used lobsters as fertilizer—designed to increase the supply of lobsters. Presently researchers are experimenting with electrical stimulation techniques to investigate spermatophore production in American lobsters, with an eye toward experimen-tal manipulation of sperm, artificial insemination, and so forth. Science, unable so far to strengthen man's ability to process waste debris without overfouling the ocean, is at least keeping an eye on new ways of strengthening fishfood populations, and for that we should all be grateful. The National Office of Sea Grants has been actively supporting the soft blue crab industry for many years, by sponsoring research in such areas as developing im-proved shelling, packaging, and marketing techniques.

Increasing the supply of lobsters has been a goal since primitive times. When Thor Heyerdahl explored Easter Island he discovered stone carvings of lobsters and was told that they "give power to actual things" (*Aku Aku*). He wrote that he was shown a "very realistic sculpture of a lobster, or to be more correct, a Pacific langouste, with its legs curved under as in nature and its feelers stretched flat along its back." He was told, "This gives power to the lobster, so that they multiply along the coast" (p. 208).

Blind as a Crayfish

When I was last in the Carlsbad Caverns in New Mexico I was overwhelmed by the enormous number of bats hanging inside, something like a hundred bats in every square foot, as I recall. I became interested in bats and even discovered that some of them have been clocked at 35 miles per hour, which is pretty amazing, particularly when we talk about being blind as a bat. More recently I have discovered that there are some species of crayfish that are blind and that *also* live in caves! In particular is the best known of the bunch, *Cambarus pellucidas*, which inhabits the Monmouth Cave of Kentucky (and to think I never saw one when I visited). In any case, feel free to call someone as "blind as a crayfish" and then be set to prove your point!

Incidentally, crayfish are not generally found along the shores of the Chesapeake and so, as one naturalist has noted, "When one is captured it becomes an object of great interest; some people wonder where the lobster came from" (J. Needham, with J. T. Lloyd, in *The Life of Inland Waters*).

Thinking Like a Crab: T. E. Lawrence's Preference

In the summer of 1988 I spent several weeks in residence at

Oxford, primarily studying Shakespeare but also spending some time looking into some famous Oxford graduates like T. E. Lawrence, who had gone off on archaeological expeditions and of course joined in the Arab revolt against the Turks, a revolt he led beautifully in his combination of being philosopher, scholar, linguist, and military tactician. In reading Lawrence's famous *Revolt in the Desert* I found him at one point describing his preferred manner of thought in the following surprising way:

"Next morning I was up early and out among Feisal's troops towards the side of Kheif, by myself, trying to feel the pulse of their opinions in a moment. Time was of the essence of my effort, for it was necessary to gain in ten days the impressions which *would ordinarily have been the fruit of weeks of observing in my crab fashion, that sideways-slipping affair of the senses.* [Italics mine.] Normally I would go along all day, with sounds immediate but blind to every detail, only generally aware that there were things red, or things grey, or clear things about me. Today my eyes had to be switched straight to my brain, that I might note a thing or two more clearly by contrast with the former mistiness" (*Revolt in the Desert*).

There is something almost perfect, for me, in Lawrence's reference to the crab. He acknowledges in a single sentence the way a crab moves around in his unusual fashion, taking things in over time. It is, I suspect, a very wise way to proceed in our general interactions with the world, doing a little bit of "sideways-slipping" so as not to rush to judgment or reveal our plans too quickly.

When Crabs Ring Ralph's Bell

My late longtime good friend on Shelter Island, Ralph Grasso, crabbed in many different ways, but one that was particularly interesting to hear about once was the "bell-ringing" method.

He would use a "killy-ring" with ten or fifteen killies tied onto a circular metal ring wired to a stake at the center with a thin wire leading up to a sleigh bell tied at the top. When the crabs would begin to tug on the killies the bells would ring, and the crabber would begin pulling in the line. It is sort of like getting a telephone call from your quarry.

Ralph also explained a method he and his father used that did not employ a bell but struck me as very ingenious. He would take a large metal ring with some chunks of bait tied to it, place it on top of the seine, and put the whole thing on the bottom, with three ropes pyramiding to a rope to close it. In other words, as a variation on a trap, the larger seine would be pulled up, bringing the bait and hopefully several crabs all at once. If you created several such net contraptions you could have one off each side of a boat, or you could walk waist-deep into a bay and throw it in front of you, give crabs time enough to find and get to the bait, thereby crawling onto the net, and then pull the whole thing up. The only problem I find with this method is that you don't have anyone ringing a bell to say, "Come and catch me."

Crabs Don't Always Get a Long Winter's Nap

Although the Bible tells us that to everything there is a season, try telling that to those who want to catch crabs off-season. Just when some crabs think they are safely bedding down for a long winter's nap, along come fishermen with dredges. Since crabs become dormant in the winter months, and really do settle down, they of course can be caught rather easily, if not always abundantly, with dredges.

In a recent discussion of "The Winter Dredge Fishery for Blue Crabs in Raritan Bay," Clyde MacKenzie notes that winter dredging for crabs in Raritan Bay has been going on steadily since the 1800s, when sailing sloops and schooners used during the season for both oystering and hard clamming were put into use for catching crabs. No point in letting boats become dormant either!

One interesting statistic is that some 70–80 percent of the crabs caught by winter dredging are females, so maybe they are deeper sleepers. MacKenzie notes that the typical dredge boat makes about ten dredges, each taking some thirty-five minutes, and catches about twenty-two crabs each dredge. It's uncertain work, but the crabs caught in the winter this way have been keeping restaurants well stocked for many years and will, in all likelihood, continue to do so far into the future. Other winter crab dredging takes place in the Delaware Bay, the Lower Chesapeake Bay, and certain North Carolina bays.*

Right-Clawed and Left-Clawed: Lobsters on the Mound

Some sea creatures rely on poisonous weapons and others on mechanical ones, the lobster's claws being one of the best examples of the latter. As is commonly known, lobsters have one very large claw, known as the crushing pincer, and one smaller known as the cutting pincer. On the large claw are the big blunter teeth and on the smaller, the sharper smaller teeth. Lobsters have been routinely observed holding down prey with the big clublike claw while slowly ripping into it with the smaller, cutting claw.

Lobsters can have the big claw on either the left or the right side, and once in a while you will come across a lobster with two cutting claws, but very rarely with two crushing claws. It should also be noted that the large claw has tremendous strength, typi-

---

*For a full discussion, see MacKenzie's article in *Underwater Naturalist*, Vol. 17, No. 4 (1988), pp. 7–10.

cally thirty times body weight in the grip (compared with man's two-thirds of body weight grip!), so whether a lefty or righty, the strength is outstanding (as discussed by F. W. Flattely et al. in *The Biology of the Sea Shore*).

The Glass Crab and Other Curious Crabs

Countless species of crabs are wonderfully different from the more familiar species we know. One is known as the glass crab because its body is completely translucent and fish look right through it without seeing it. Who could ask for a better protection? Some crabs travel on turtles' backs, others live in the folds of jellyfish, one in the inside of a sea cucumber and another inside the Brazilian starfish. Some crabs, including the Grapsus, go successfully after birds in their nests! Some land crabs in the West Indies wreak havoc on sugarcane plantations, while others expertly open coconuts. A few are long-distance swimmers, like Henslow's swimming crab, which apparently is often seen "many miles from land [and] will dart into a school of herrings, seize a fish in its knife-like claws, and cling to it until its victim floats dead upon the surface" (J. W. Buel, *Sea and Land*).

Catching Lobsters with Feet and Torches

Thor Heyerdahl's Easter Island explorations not only introduced him to using stone carvings of lobsters to increase their ability to multiply, but also gave him a feeling for catching lobsters with feet, and using not flashlights as we do for night blue-crabbing, but torches. Here is the account:

"When the appointed evening approached, the sea was calm and glassy. Some of our men had been out by moonlight the night before catching rock lobster with native girl friends. This was one of the island's great delicacies: it is really a big lobster without claws. Our frogmen would often spear it in underwater caves, but the simplest way was to wade breast-high in the water along the shore at night with flaming torches. The native vahines were very skillful at this. They trod on the great creatures and held them fast with their toes till they could plunge down to pick them up and put them in a sack" (*Aku Aku*, p. 278). That night they had over twenty lobsters at a fiesta, along with fresh pineapple. I have gone *clamming* with my feet but foot-lobstering is, as it were, a new twist!

Lobsters in the Movies

It's always fun to do a computer search on a topic like this. I won't try to tell you about every last item I tracked down. Take note, though, of *It Happened to Jane: Twinkle and Shine*, a 1959 Columbia Pictures movie starring Doris Day and Jack Lemmon running a lobster business despite villainous interference from Ernie Kovacs. Then there is *Leonard Part 6* written by and starring Bill Cosby (1987) as a retired spy. His purpose is to save the world from a crazy villainess (Gloria Foster) and her avenging frogs, fish, cats, and, yes, lobsters! And for those who like their horror movies with a bit of zip in them, how about *The Tingler*, a 1959 Vincent Price film for which "Percepto" vibrators were placed under the viewers' seats to produce feelings of fright as Dr. Chapin, played by Price (a fellow Yaleman, I should note), battled a lobsterlike creature to protect a mute girl. I won't even tell you what the computer came up with for crabs at the cinema!

Now, That's Impossible

We have coined, over the centuries, many expressions to describe the impossible. Typical is Pindar's "the sands of the sea—who can number them?" One less common phrase you might wish to try out hails from about 200 B.C. in the writing of Naevius: *"Prius pariet locusta Lucam bovem."* If you are hesitant to use the Latin, translate to: "Sooner will a lobster spawn a Lucanian cow," or simply, "That's as unlikely as a lobster giving birth to a cow."

Another Kind of "Blue Crab"

Dr. Warren Rathjen, marine adviser at the Brevard Service Complex in Melbourne, Florida, has brought to my attention for this trivia chapter specifically the little-known fact that there is more than one variety of the blue crab along the eastern U.S. coasts. Warren caught one and sent it to the National Marine Fisheries Service in Washington (you can always send a specimen there) and learned that he had caught "a *Callinectes bocourti* A. Milne Edwards." It turns out that the usual range for this species is Jamaica and Belize to southern Brazil, but, as they wrote from Washington, "there are scattered records from southern Mississippi, the Indian River region of Florida, now yours, and South Carolina." The "now yours" note is a welcome comment to any beach and ocean lover, and as the reply continued, "marginal records are always welcome additions to a biological and biogeographic information. I will put this specimen, fragmented though it is, in the USNMN collection. Positive evidence is always better than a mere record." In addition to letting us know about another blue crab coming up our way, the incident reminds us once again that there is much that we do not know about the ocean, its inhabitants, their ways, and their traffic patterns.

Suggested
Further Reading

DURING THE COURSE OF researching, writing, and revising this book I have benefited from a great many reference works and books of a more specialized nature. There are some that will be of particular interest to those readers who want to pursue lobsters and crabs further.

There are six books I would recommend highly, beginning with William Warner's *Beautiful Swimmers: Watermen, Crabs and the Chesapeake Bay* (first published by Little, Brown in 1976 and available as a Penguin paperback). The others are: Richard Headstrom's *All About Lobsters, Crabs, Shrimps and Their Relatives* (N.Y., 1979; available in a 1985 Dover paperback); Edward R. Ricciuti's *Secrets of Potfishing* (Hancock House paperback, 1982); Jim Capossela's *How to Catch Crabs by the Bushel! The Manual of Sport Crabbing* (paperback, 1984, Northeast Sportsman's Press);

Lynette L. Walther's *The Art of Catching and Cooking Crabs* (1983, Sussex Prints, Inc.); and Cy and Pat Liberman's *The Crab Book* (1978 paperback, The Middle Atlantic Press). The last five of these books are wonderful to read, informative, and blend how-to with cookery.

Of a more general nature but valuable for any sea creature lover's bookshelf are: Kenneth L. Gosner, *A Field Guide to the Atlantic Seashore* (Boston, 1979; part of the Houghton Mifflin Peterson Field Guide Series); John Crompton's *The Sea* (first published in 1957, republished in 1988 by Nick Lyons Books); William H. Amos and Stephen H. Amos, *Atlantic and Gulf Coasts* (Alfred A. Knopf, 1985; an Audubon Society Nature Guide); Augusta Foote Arnold's *The Sea-Beach at Ebb-Tide* (originally published in 1901 by The Century Company, and republished by Dover in 1968); and Philip Kopper's *The Wild Edge: Life and Lore of the Great Atlantic Beaches* (first published by Time Books, 1979; republished by Penguin Books, 1981).

A wonderful book about lobstering is Louise Dickinson Rich's *The Peninsula* (J. B. Lippincott Co., N.Y., 1958) and another is *The Salt Brook* (Anchor Books, N.Y., 1977, written by a group of Maine high school students with their teacher Pamela Wood's guidance). There are some wonderful anecdotes as well in Rich's *State O' Maine* (N.Y., 1964).

Three books of general interest that I found interesting are Robert D. Ballard, et al., *The Ocean Realm* (prepared by the Special Publications Division of the National Geographic Society in 1979, Washington, D.C.); Gardner Soule's *Wide Ocean: Discoveries at Sea* (Rand McNally, N.Y., 1970); and G. E. MacGintie and Nettie MacGintie, *Natural History of Marine Animals* (McGraw-Hill, N.Y., 1949).

The many wonderful seafood cookbooks I have consulted have been mentioned in the text and certainly all of them are recommended. If you love eating seafood, it is hard to find a cookbook in that area that you won't like!

Appendix: Shellfish Regulatory Agencies

Contact one of the following agencies for information concerning regulations governing the taking of crabs and lobsters in your state.

Alabama Department of Conservation
  and Natural Resources
Game and Fish Division
64 North Union Street
Montgomery, AL 36130
(334) 242-3465 or 220-3465
James D. Martin, Commissioner

Alaska Department of Fish and Game
P.O. Box 2256
Juneau, AK 99802-5526
(907) 465-4100
Frank Rue, Commissioner

California Department of Fish and Game
1416 9th Street—Room 1320
Sacramento, CA 95814
Robert Treanor, Executive Director,
    Fish and Game Commission

State of Connecticut
Department of Environmental Protection
79 Elm Street
Hartford, CT 06106-5127
Arthur J. Rocque, Commissioner

Delaware Division of Fish & Wildlife
89 Kings Highway
Dover, DE 19901
(302) 739-5297
Andrew T. Manus, Director

Georgia Department of Natural Resources
Law Enforcement
Coastal Resources Division
One Conservation Way
Brunswick, GA 31523
(912) 264-7237

Louisiana Department of Wildlife and Fisheries
Enforcement Division
P.O. Box 98000
Baton Rouge, LA 70898-9000
(504) 765-2469
Major Keith LaCaze, Public Information Officer

Florida Division of Marine Resources
Department of Environmental Protection
Room 843
3900 Commonwealth Boulevard
Tallahassee, FL 32303
(850) 488-6058

Maine Department of Marine Resources
Hallowell—21 State House Station
Augusta, ME 04333-0021
(207) 624-6550
Fax (207) 624-6024

Maryland Department of Natural Resources
580 Taylor Avenue
Tawes State Office Building
Annapolis, MD 21401
(410) 260-8250
Dorothy Leonard, Director, Fisheries Service

Massachusetts Department of Fisheries,
    Wildlife, and Environmental Law Enforcement
Division of Marine Fisheries
Leverett Saltonstall Building, Government Center
100 Cambridge Street, Room 1901
Boston, MA 02202
(617) 727-3193
Philip Coates, Director

Michigan Department of Natural Resources
Fisheries Division
530 West Allegan Street
P.O. Box 30028
Lansing, MI 48909
(517) 373-3375
Fax (517) 373-0381
Kelley Smith, Division Chief

New Hampshire Fish & Game Department
Law Enforcement Division
2 Hazen Drive
Concord, NH 03301-6500
(603) 271-3127

New Jersey Department of Environmental Protection
401 East State Street
7th Floor, East Wing
P.O. Box 402
Trenton, NJ 08625-0402
(609) 292-2885
Fax (609) 292-7695

New York State Department of Environmental
    Conservation
Office of Natural Resources
Division of Fish, Wildlife, and Marine Resources
50 Wolf Road
Albany, NY 12233
(518) 457-5690
Gerry Barnhart, Director

North Carolina Department of Environmental
   and Natural Resources
Division of Marine Fisheries
3441 Arendell Street
Morehead City, NC 28557
(252) 726-7021

Oregon Department of Fish and Wildlife
Fish Division
2501 Southwest 1st Avenue
Portland, OR 97207
(503) 872-5252
Shellfish regulations (541) 867-4741
Jim Greer, Director

Rhode Island Division of Environmental Management
Division of Fish and Wildlife
4808 Tower Hill Road
Wakefield, RI 02879
(401) 222-3075 or 789-3094
John Stolgitis, Chief

South Carolina Department of Natural Resources
Marine Resource Division
Office of Fisheries Management, Shellfish Management Program
217 Fort Johnson Road
P.O. Box 12599
Charleston, SC 29412
John Miglarese, Deputy Director

Texas Parks and Wildlife Department
Coastal Fishing Division
4200 Smith School Road
Austin, TX 78744
(512) 389-4800

Virginia Marine Resources Commission
P.O. Box 756
2600 Washington Avenue
Newport News, VA 23607-0756
(757) 247-2200

Washington Department of Fish and Wildlife
Natural Resource Building
1121 Washington Street, S.E.
Olympia, WA 98501
(360) 902-2200
Fax (360) 902-2230

Index